George Orwell Studies

Volume Three

No. 2

George Orwell

Publishing Office
Abramis Academic
ASK House
Northgate Avenue
Bury St. Edmunds
Suffolk
IP32 6BB
UK

Tel: +44 (0)1284 700321
Fax: +44 (0)1284 717889
Email: info@abramis.co.uk
Web: www.abramis.co.uk

Copyright
All rights reserved. No part of this publication may be reproduced in any material form (including photocopying or storing it in any medium by electronic means, and whether or not transiently or incidentally to some other use of this publication) without the written permission of the copyright owner, except in accordance with the provisions of the Copyright, Designs and Patents Act 1988, or under terms of a licence issued by the Copyright Licensing Agency Ltd, 33-34, Alfred Place, London WC1E 7DP, UK. Applications for the copyright owner's permission to reproduce part of this publication should be addressed to the Publishers.

© 2019 George Orwell Studies & Abramis Academic

ISSN 2399-1267
ISBN 978-1-84549-742-2

George Orwell Studies

Contents

Editorial
Humour beyond the Gloom of *Nineteen Eighty-Four* – by Richard Lance Keeble — Page 3

Nineteen Eighty-Four and Me
An Invitation to Big Brother – by Ron Bateman — Page 6

George Orwell and the Millennial Whoop? The Enduring Relevance of the Music of *Nineteen Eighty-Four* – by Carol Biederstadt — Page 15

Child Lore in *Nineteen Eighty-Four* – by Kristin Bluemel — Page 23

'23-F' vs '24-F': On Learning about Orwell at a Momentous Time in Spanish History – by Jesús Isaías Gómez López — Page 29

(Close) Encounters with George? – by John Rodden — Page 31

Patriarchal Norms and Sexual Desire in Michael Radford's Film of *Nineteen Eighty-Four* – by Martin Stollery — Page 36

Who was Julia? *Nineteen Eighty-Four*'s Many Heroines – by D. J. Taylor — Page 39

Articles
Names in *Burmese Days*: A Fantasia – by Douglas Kerr — Page 44

Orwell and Captain Robinson's 'Poet': A More Than Cautionary Note – by Phil Baker — Page 47

Orwell in Paris: Who Was Ruth Graves? – by Darcy Moore — Page 55

Gordon Bowker: So Wonderfully Insightful into Orwell the Man and his Writings – by Richard Lance Keeble — Page 71

Reviews
Peter Mitchell on *Between the Bullet and the Lie: Essays on Orwell*, by Kristian Williams; Simon Goulding on *George Orwell on Screen*, by David Ryan; Megan Faragher on *The Politics of 1930s British Literature: Education, Class, Gender*, by Natasha Periyan, and Matthew Chambers on *George Orwell Illustrated*, by David Smith, Mike Mosher (illus.) — Page 77

Re-evaluations
Tombs: Sharing Orwell's Penchant for Puncturing Shibboleths – by Darcy Moore — Page 89

Editors
Richard Lance Keeble — University of Lincoln
Tim Crook — Goldsmiths, University of London

Reviews Editor
Luke Seaber — University College London

Production Editor
Paul Anderson — University of Essex

Editorial Board
Kristin Bluemel — Monmouth University, New Jersey
Peter Marks — University of Sydney
John Newsinger — Bath Spa University
Marina Remy — Paris Sorbonne
Jean Seaton — University of Westminster
Peter Stansky — Stanford University, US
D. J. Taylor — Author, journalist, biographer of Orwell
Florian Zollmann — Newcastle University

EDITORIAL

Humour beyond the Gloom of *Nineteen Eighty-Four*

RICHARD LANCE KEEBLE

To mark the 70th anniversary of the publication of George Orwell's classic dystopian novel, this issue begins with a section titled '*Nineteen Eighty-Four* and Me'. The fascinating and varied contributions from an international group of scholars – Ron Bateman, Carol Biederstadt, Kristin Bluemel, Jesús Isaías Gómez López, John Rodden, Martin Stollery and D. J. Taylor – mix the personal, reflective, the biographical, the political and the theoretical.

The novel is normally associated with the doom and gloom of the oppressive, authoritarian, Big Brother society. Yet the more I personally dip into the novel the more its humorous elements impress: indeed, ironic and satiric humour runs right through it. After all, the Ministry of Truth disseminates lies, the Ministry of Love is where Winston Smith is tortured, the Ministry of Peace concerns itself only with war while the Ministry of Plenty is involved with the rationing of food. Bernard Crick, in one of the most perceptive analyses of the novel, talks of it as being inspired by 'satiric rage' (2007: 147). He identifies seven broad satiric themes:

- the division of the world at Tehran by Stalin, Roosevelt and Churchill;
- the mass media and proletarisation (now termed 'dumbing down');
- power-hunger and totalitarianism – particularly in the depiction of the torturer O'Brien who is shown driven mad by power-hunger;
- the corruption of language in the drive towards Newspeak;
- the destruction of any objective history and truth by the Ministry of Truth;
- the view (well-known at Orwell's time) of James Burnham (1941) that capitalism and communism will converge through managerialism.

Crick argues convincingly (ibid: 148-149) that the novel is 'plainly a satire on hierarchical societies in general'. 'Orwell's satire is so consistent that the dictator is actually called "Big Brother". "Big Brother is watching you," but not watching over you as a brother should.'

Moreover, too many commentaries (and film and stage adaptations) on *Nineteen Eighty-Four* regard it as concluding with the anti-hero Winston Smith loving Big Brother. But, in fact, Orwell cleverly adds an Appendix titled 'The Principles of Newspeak' in which he brilliantly deconstructs the very language he has invented (Keeble 2015: 16). And the Appendix offers a far from pessimistic ending. For here we are told that translations into Newspeak of writers such as Shakespeare, Milton, Swift, Byron and Dickens were going so slowly that the 'final adoption of Newspeak had been fixed for late a date as 2010'. Just before the end, there is even a quotation from the American Declaration of Independence! As Crick concludes (2007: 158): 'If we read *Nineteen Eighty-Four* as Swiftian satire, this is as good to say "this year, next year, sometimes, never". Colloquial language, the common people and common sense will survive the most resolute attempts at total control.'

There is also satiric humour in Orwell's decision to give the room where Winston is tortured the number 101 – after his office at 55 Portland Place, London, where he worked for the BBC's Eastern Service from 1941-1942 (Meyers 2000: 214). Bowker (2003) also reflects on the fact that the name of O'Brien happened to be the codename of Hugh O'Donnell, the KGB handler of David Crook who was keeping a close eye on Orwell in Spain (Keeble 2012: 154). He concludes that Orwell was oblivious to this and so 'the fact that the character in *Nineteen Eighty-Four* who first wins the confidence of Winston Smith and then betrays him is given the name O'Brien must be one of the strangest coincidences in literature' (op cit: 219). But Orwell had close connections with the spooks and probably went to the continent in 1945 as part of some kind of intelligence mission for David Astor (Keeble 2012). So he may well have found out this information about O'Donnell through his contacts. If so – this is a wonderful satiric jibe.

Humour permeates so much of Orwell's writings – in, for instance, many of his 'As I Please' columns in *Tribune* (1943-1947), in his celebration of the sexy, seaside postcards of Donald McGill (1941) and in his essays 'Dickens' (1940), 'Some thoughts on the common toad' (1946), 'Funny not vulgar (1945) and 'Lear, Tolstoy and the Fool' (1947) (see Keeble 2015). In fact, he may even be considered one of the greatest (though largely unacknowledged) humourists of the English language. It is not surprising then that humour should be such an intrinsic element of his masterpiece of 1949.

- This issue carries the first essay of a new 'Re-evaluations' section, to be co-ordinated by Darcy Moore, which will look at texts published in the past (and too often ignored) which provide important insights into Orwell's life and writings. Here, the spotlight is on *The English and Their History: The First Thirteen Centuries* (2014), by Robert Tombs.

- Following the decision of Prof. John Newsinger to step down (for personal reasons) from jointly editing *George Orwell Studies*, I'm delighted to announce that Prof. Tim Crook has taken on this role. Tim has published widely on Orwell and organises the annual symposium at Goldsmiths, University of London. His knowledge, contacts and wit will all, I am sure, play crucial roles in the development of the journal.

REFERENCES

Bowker, Gordon (2003) *George Orwell*, London: Little, Brown

Crick, Bernard (2007) *Nineteen Eighty-Four*: Context and controversy, Rodden, John (ed.) *The Cambridge Companion to George Orwell*, Cambridge: Cambridge University Press pp 146-159

Keeble, Richard Lance (2012) Orwell, *Nineteen Eighty-Four* and the spooks, Keeble, Richard Lance (ed.) *Orwell Today*, Bury St Edmunds: Abramis pp 151-163

Keeble, Richard Lance (2015) 'There is always room for one more custard pie': Orwell's humour, Keeble, Richard Lance and Swick, David (eds) *Pleasures of the Prose*: *Journalism and Humour*, Bury St Edmunds, Abramis pp 10-25

Meyers, Jeffrey (2000) *Orwell: Wintry Conscience of a Generation*, New York/London: W. W. Norton and Company Ltd

NINETEEN EIGHTY-FOUR AND ME

An Invitation to Big Brother

RON BATEMAN

The future world that Orwell imagined in *Nineteen Eighty-Four* did not appear realised during its prophetic year, except maybe within the barbed-wire confinement of Europe's Eastern Bloc. The fact that it had yet to materialise in the West was largely put down to the resilience of the 'democratic spirit' and the enduring balance of power between executive, legislative and judicial institutions (McGinn 1983: 67-75). If we move the clock about a decade-and-a-half forward an unparalleled age of technological advancement is now in motion; this at a time when the Western democracies are struggling to come to grips with an alarming increase in terrorist activity. Suddenly the relevance of Orwell's dystopian novel is re-emerging; mainly because it is a commonly held view that the introduction of state-sponsored surveillance into people's everyday lives is a distinctly 'Orwellian' measure. What is less clear are the 'Orwellian dangers' that we expose ourselves to in the course of our everyday online activities, in particular our exposure to the commercially-sponsored information gathering capability that exists within our computers – not to mention our everyday exposure to a plethora of fake news articles.

ENHANCED SURVEILLANCE

Orwell was not too wide of the mark with regard to his warnings about the future supremacy of state-sponsored surveillance. In 1994, a typical large city such as Liverpool boasted 28 very basic CCTV cameras in its centre. By 2002 it had installed 240 high-definition, digital cameras interconnected with 70 miles of fibre-optic cable – each capable of reading a car number-plate from over half a mile away, a measure that enabled a million square metres of the city centre to be closely scrutinised – its activities watched, recorded and logged around the clock (Addley 2002). By the same year in the UK as a whole, the surveillance industry (private investigators, credit agencies and security services) employed more than a million people and Britons were the most heavily scrutinised people on earth (ibid). In the immediate aftermath of 9/11, technology was advancing with such alarming speed that surveillance experts were suddenly seeing through walls using a technique called electromagnetic radiation, and listening in on conversations without need of a 'bug' – a simple laser beam aimed at a window that could easily magnify the vibrations caused by the voices inside (Branigan 2002).

Two decades on from those advancements, so desensitised have we become that we carry on with our everyday lives largely indifferent to the sheer density of surveillance technology around us – a world in which CCTV monitors our every move outside of our private space. Unless it is one's intention to break the law, few people appear to worry about the intrusiveness of surveillance hardware, and express fascination that there are satellites above us that can now reproduce images of such amazingly high resolution as to identify an object ten centimetres in length (Dickerson 2015). We probably worry more about our smartphone location being tracked with pin-point accuracy – allowing our whereabouts to be known to all manner of crime-busting agencies – or even our partners! We retain this indifference to surveillance so long as it does not invade our private space – the sanctity of our own homes, or even our inner minds. The problem is that the majority of us are now tech-savvy – we like to do everything on-line with the minimum of fuss – meaning we choose a recordable electronic pathway to make our choices, rather than a verbal one. We are also all social animals who want to get a hearing, and by embracing the confessional culture that is a key part of social media, we are inadvertently encouraging Big Brother into the sanctuary of our inner space.

THE ONLINE REVOLUTION

The debate surrounding the validity of Orwell's warnings in the computer age tends to focus on the nature of the relationship between the computer and the individual. Rather than being that of master and servant, as Orwell predicted, it is suggested that computerised surveillance is more integrated with commerce – something that Orwell did not foresee (Marks 2014). While Marks's suggestion is certainly true of the internet age, we may not have become servants or slaves to the computers in the traditional sense. Rather it appears we have become addicted, whether via gambling, gaming, surfing or social networking, and we feel deprived of our connection to the world without these devices. When one enters a railway carriage and sees fourteen of the sixteen occupants staring into small screens, we see an image of a society that has grown dependent on data uploads throughout every waking hour.

The cost to the addicted user is difficult to fathom since, for many people, the devices have replaced books; for others, verbal or face-to-face communication. For just about everyone they have stolen away precious time that people would once have spent alone with their private thoughts, and the surveillance element utilises that time to extract as much information from us as possible. One might be inclined to question the claim that Orwell was completely wrong in his master-slave relationship between the person and the telescreen (Huber 2015), particularly if we view the current relationship as being one of dependency or addiction.

The information highway we refer to as the internet has very quickly emerged as the primary source of communication between individuals, and individuals and businesses. In amongst its users are large corporations that are able to build huge databases of information on every individual who ever dared to click a mouse. The covert information-gathering aspect of this surveillance monster has created an intricate system of algorithms that know us better than we know ourselves. It is chilling to think about how much is known about us by corporations that are busy compiling extraordinarily detailed databases of our everyday actions, or distributing parcels of data to be scrutinised by hundreds of different organisations.

As far back as 2002, details of the average economically active adult were already located in around 700 databases – a formidable reference book for each person (Davies 2002). From the moment we embraced the potential of our electronic devices, they have been disseminating all manner of data to unknown receivers to be routinely scanned and profiled. Simply sending an email is no more private than mailing a handwritten letter beneath the gaze of the secret police, and to use the internet is likely to put your privacy at the mercy of the state for several months. Even before the smart-TV revolution, cable TV companies required users to hook-up the set top-box to a telephone line to enable them to track what their subscribers were up to, and to log detailed information. Every choice the subscriber made is fed back down to the digital TV firm's headquarters, enabling them to target advertisements more efficiently. The information could thereafter potentially be sold to other companies (Steinberg 2014).

The internet equivalent in Orwell's fictional society of Airstrip One is the *telescreen* – like the internet, this is a two-way audio-visual system that gathers information through surveillance, rather than electronic mail, and directly disseminates fake-news to the masses for the purpose of maintaining the status quo. In today's world, the ease with which fake news can be disseminated on a grand scale is truly frightening. The possibility that such methods had been employed to skew the result of the 2016 US presidential election, and possibly even the Brexit referendum of the same year, have been well documented. Those among us who participate in posting opinions on closed or admin-controlled discussion groups can appreciate how a site such as Facebook can very easily become the perfect totalitarian tool. For example, one group boasting hundreds of thousands of subscribers recently posted the claim that the German city of Nuremberg was not bombed during World War Two. When I pointed out to them that it was an accepted fact that 90 per cent of the city centre was destroyed by allied bombing, my comment was removed. Later, when I contacted them to suggest that it was wholly inaccurate for them to suggest that the US had refused entry to the diarist Anna Frank before her family went into hiding, I was excluded from commenting further on the page altogether. For a generation that internalises the majority of its information via the internet, how simple it can be for lies to pass into history if this practice were allowed to continue unchallenged.

THE HIDDEN DANGERS OF SOCIAL MEDIA

Social media has also become the harbinger of the Orwellian concept of thought-crime. Law enforcement agencies and the intelligence community were quick to spot the surveillance potential of online devices. In 2000, the Regulation of Investigatory Powers Act handed police and government agencies extensive powers to intercept communications on their own authority. Following 9/11 when the need for greater surveillance was at its height, government opposition to blanket communications data retention was virtually abandoned. Within three months of the atrocity, the Anti-Terrorism Crime and Security Act (2001) required all telephone and internet companies to store records of all their customers for many years. Thereafter, officers of superintendent or equivalent rank were enabled to access the information without any need for judicial or executive warrant – even for minor investigations. Think how easily these powers could eventually lead to 'grudge fishing expeditions' against innocent civilians. Even everyday social media participants can very easily find themselves hauled in front of a judge for stating an off-the-cuff remark that is deemed to fall outside of the accepted code (Casciani 2017). Powers to enforce the retention of communications data were further broadened by the Investigatory Powers Act of 2016.[1]

For civil liberties advocates – those groups who rallied against the intrusion of Big Brother, 9/11 unleashed the perfect storm. Overnight, years of hard-won reforms were abandoned and replaced with a wide range of intrusive measures to assist the eavesdroppers and spies – namely America's National Security Agency (NSA) and the United Kingdom's Government Communications Headquarters (GCHQ). Since the start of the 21st century, GCHQ has had the capacity to intercept every mobile phone in Britain and then, by using computers called 'ECHELON Dictionaries', automatically search through millions of intercepts for 'keywords' (Greisler and Stupak 2006). Additional powers to include the prevention and detection of serious crime were already available courtesy of the Intelligence Services Act of 1994 (MacAskill et al. 2013). The protection of personal privacy now seems virtually impossible.

RON BATEMAN THE VALIDITY OF INTELLIGENCE

The truly worrying thing about the extended power of intelligence gathering agencies is their ability to destroy a person's life, particularly in instances where intelligence takes the wrong path. Just over a decade after Orwell's *Nineteen Eighty-Four* was published in 1949, a communications intelligence agreement was signed linking the 'Five Eyes' nations (Australia, Canada, New Zealand, the UK and USA) into the secret eavesdropping agreement we now know as Echelon. Defenders cited its capacity to listen-in on missile deals being brokered in many volatile regions of the world. Since its inception, Echelon has morphed into an eavesdropping Big Brother 'monster' that has effectively become a law unto itself in its mission to rule the airwaves and cyberspace by piecing together snippets of information – effectively joining up the dots. But the dots do not always get joined-up correctly: since 9/11, it has been reported that some people have found themselves added to a list of potential terrorists on the strength of an ambiguous word used in a phone call to a friend (Bamford 2002). We can see how, in contrast to Orwell's Big-Brother, today's surveillance no longer targets specific individuals or groups – rather it profiles millions of people at a time. Also these modern information systems are now generally operable with other systems, there being no barriers to sharing information. Data that would have taken years to compile is now available in seconds.

Intriguingly, Orwell failed to foresee the significance of DNA in the profiling of individuals – the probability that the biggest threat to our privacy lies within us. DNA is like an identity card that every person carries around with them from birth, all the time shedding bits of it wherever they go. Your DNA can verify where you were, what you did, and even what you may become. Home Office statistics indicate that the UK National Criminal Intelligence DNA Database set up in 1995 now has samples from around six million crime suspects, and by 2007 was reportedly growing by 30,000 samples each month.[2]

Surveillance technology is also being increasingly used in workplaces. All the while workers are logging on to their computers, corporate information technology departments can watch each and every action they make. Corporate PC stations might give the user the impression that they are in control, just as though they were on their own home PC, but in reality it is usually connected to a central server that tracks every piece of data that travels through the network. Even deleted emails will be recorded somewhere on a central database. Internet and email gives employers the most powerful tool for monitoring the activities of their staff, endowing them with great powers – particularly those looking to get rid of certain staff members. Similarly, swipe-cards on entrances and workstations have allowed employers to follow the movements of their employees and to log how much time is spent in certain areas of the building. Companies also use special investigators to vet the CVs of job applicants. Prospective employees are commonly asked to sign an authorisation that allows the investigators to dig deep into their background.[3]

THE VALUE OF INFORMATION

The price that private companies are prepared to pay for information has also added to the surveillance boom and extended the invitation of Big Brother into our private space. Everyday consumer transactions generate a new trail of data that is recorded, analysed and added to profiles on thousands of private sector databases. Spending habits are now a commodity in their own right valued in the billions of pounds, while profiling – the merging of information from various lists – can lead to a very detailed picture of a person. Those in search of easy credit are particularly vulnerable. Experian built a billion-dollar business around data collection and are now the biggest credit-checking organisation in the world – holding detailed information on over one billion people, vehicles and businesses in the US alone (Experian 2017). Aside from credit checks, it also investigates individuals and businesses on behalf the police, social security officials and companies seeking background checks on prospective employees. It is also the suppliers who have invested heavily in advanced surveillance systems that are driving the market – desperate to sell their innovations, while at the same time governments are crying out for more sophisticated technologies in the fight against terrorism. It has been argued that the growth of the surveillance state is merely a classic example of the power of marketing (Collins 2002).

One additional question that needs to be asked is: 'Now that we have inadvertently encouraged Big Brother into the deepest parts of our private world via our online activities, are we happy for the intelligence gathered to be used to our advantage?' A study of Facebook use concluded that after a very short period of 'liking' various posts, the social media giant will know you better than anyone else in your circle – even better than you know yourself in many cases (Harari 2015: 396-397). The implications of this in Harari's view is that people might soon abandon their own psychological judgements and rely on computers when making important life decisions – such as career paths and even choosing partners. The amount of medical information on each of us stored in vast databanks will certainly be used to our advantage. A family doctor, for example, can only ever know a fraction of the information required to diagnose a condition, whereas artificial intelligence can not only store the patient's medical history, but also information on any number of known conditions and research updates on those conditions; in short, it can diagnose far more accurately than your family doctor. In San Francisco, a pharmacy opened that was run by a single robot dispensing prescriptions with 100 per cent accuracy – compared to 98.3 percent accuracy of its flesh-and-blood equivalent (ibid: 366-369).

CONCLUSION

It appears as though our online activities have desensitised us to Orwell's warning about the loss of privacy – something that is central to the freedom and autonomy of every individual. This is particularly worrying, for if we gathered together all the information that government, police and privately-run agencies hold on us, we would suddenly feel as though our freedom were gravely at risk. 'Privacy is like oxygen; we only really appreciate it when it's gone,' wrote Charles Sykes in *The End of Privacy*: 'The internet has rewritten the rules of private and public life, providing an illusion of privacy in a realm that is actually a goldfish bowl' (Sykes 1999). Through our obsessive use of online devices, we are gradually eroding that privacy without realising it. Similarly, social media has afforded us an easy platform to air our innermost thoughts on the public stage – an indication that privacy has now largely become a discarded value. The linkage of almost every surveillance initiative to national security and the fight against terrorism has made it very difficult for civil liberties campaigners to argue for increased protection of private lives. The sheer pace of surveillance innovation and the nature and extent of the privacy invasion has outrun the capacity of the law to provide limitations.

One final thought: as accurate as Orwell's warning has become, I have always felt that a far more credible and hence scary vision of the future was provided by the Tony Scott spy thriller film, *Enemy of the State* (1998). The screenwriter, David Marconi, provided a frightening portrayal of the modern surveillance state, and a scenario in which a targeted individual could only obtain privacy by mingling with the crowds in a public place. The US National Security Agency was quick to make the statement that the surveillance possibilities outlined in the film were fiction, a claim that was seriously questioned in 2013 following the revelations by NSA whistleblower Edward Snowden.[4]

NOTES

[1] The Secretary of State was empowered to require telecommunications operators to retain relevant data for a number of purposes – including national security, crime prevention, and public safety. See https://assets.publishing.service.gov.uk/government/uploads/system/uploads/attachment_data/file/473745/Factsheet-Internet_Connection_Records.pdf, accessed on 24 February 2019

[2] The UK National DNA Database was set up in 1995. By 2016 it held 5.86 million profiles. National DNA Database statistics, Q1 2015-2016. See https://www.gov.uk/government/statistics/national-dna-database-statistics, accessed on 18 February 2019. In 2007, it was also reported that the database was growing at 30,000 samples each month. All UK must be on DNA database,

BBC, September 2007. See http://news.bbc.co.uk/2/hi/uk/6979138.stm, accessed on 18 February 2019

[3] Experian are one of a number of credit agencies which offer pre-employment background checks – including a prospective employee's right to work, criminal records and adverse financial checks. See https://www.experian.co.uk/background-checking/pre-employment-screening.html, accessed on 24 February 2019

[4] In 2013, former CIA contractor Edward Snowden leaked details of the US surveillance programme PRISM in which the National Security Agency (NSA) was illegally tapping into the servers of nine major internet providers and collecting telephone records of tens of millions of Americans. The agency was also shown to have electronically eavesdropped on major political figures throughout the world. See Edward Snowden: Leaks that exposed US spy programme, BBC News, 17 January 2014. Available online at https://www.bbc.com/news/world-us-canada-23123964, accessed on 18 February 2019

REFERENCES

Addley, E. (2002) Why the cameras love us – the secret state and assault on privacy, *Guardian*, 14 September

Bamford, J. (2002) *Body of Secrets: How America's NSA & Britain's GCHQ Eavesdrop on the World,* London: Arrow

Branigan, T. (2002) The eavesdroppers – the secret state and assault on privacy, *Guardian* Big Brother Supplement, 14 September

Collins, T. (2002) Mandarins and technocrats – the secret state and assault on privacy, *Guardian* Big Brother Supplement, 14 September

Davies, S. (2002) Private virtue – somebody somewhere is watching you, *Guardian*, 7 September

Dickerson, K. (2015) Companies want to launch satellites that can see a phone in your hand from space. Available online at https://www.businessinsider.com.au/satellite-image-resolution-keeps-improving-2015-10, accessed on 21 February 2019

Greisler, D. S. and Stupak R. J. (2006) *Handbook of Technology Management in Public Administration*, Abingdon: Routledge

Harari, Y. N. (2015) *Homo Deus – A Brief History of Tomorrow*, London: Vintage

Huber, P. (2015) *Orwell's Revenge: The 1984 Palimpsest,* New York: Free Press

MacAskill, E., Borger, J., Hopkins, N., Davies, N. and Ball, J. (2013) The legal loopholes that allow GCHQ to spy on the world, *Guardian*, 21 June. Available online at https://www.theguardian.com/uk/2013/jun/21/legal-loopholes-gchq-spy-world, accessed on 7 March 2019

Marks, P. (2013) Not even George Orwell envisaged this, *sydney.edu.au/news*. Available online at http://sydney.edu.au/news/84.html?newsstoryid=11808, accessed on 24 February 2019

McGinn, R. E. (1993) The politics of technology and the technology of politics, Stansky, P. (ed.) *On Nineteen Eighty-Four*, Stanford California: The Stanford Alumni Association

Steinberg, J. (2014) These devices may be spying on you (even in your own home), *forbes.com*, 27 January. Available online at https://www.forbes.com/sites/josephsteinberg/2014/01/27/these-devices-may-be-spying-on-you-even-in-your-own-home/#e29ce12b859c, accessed on 18 February 2019

Sykes, C. (1999) *The End of Privacy*, New York: St Martin's Press

RON BATEMAN NOTE ON THE CONTRIBUTOR

Ron Bateman in a founder member of The Orwell Society. He was appointed honourable secretary during the society's formative years, before taking over the editorship of the society's *Journal* from 2011 until 2016. His latest work *Rifleman of the Raj – A Soldier's Journal: British India 1919-1920* was published in 2018. He lives in Paciano, Italy.

George Orwell and the Millennial Whoop?

The Enduring Relevance of the Music of *Nineteen Eighty-Four*

CAROL BIEDERSTADT

'There seems to be a consensus that Orwell had a tin ear when it came to music,' a friend said recently, and the experts apparently agree. Orwell biographer D. J. Taylor, for example, says: 'The creator of Winston Smith, Julia and Big Brother was not, the evidence insists, a great one for music,' rightly pointing out that references to music in Orwell's 'compendious 20-volume collected works tend to cover comic songs heard on the music-hall stage, or popular ballads recalled from childhood, in which the song is somehow less important than the mental atmosphere it conjures back into life' (2005).

His assessment is valid and, without doubt, references to music in *Nineteen Eighty-Four* may at first seem to do little more than call to mind a mental atmosphere only peripheral to the plot.[1] Yet one would be mistaken to trivialise the importance of music in the novel, for though it plays but a small role, it is one of decided importance. Re-evaluating the music of the novel from a current perspective is arguably even more intriguing. While Orwell may not have been musical, prescient he patently was. Like so many other things he unerringly envisioned about the future, the popular songs favoured by the proles of his world of *Nineteen Eighty-Four* bear many striking similarities to the tunes transmitted to the masses today. This brief survey will, thus, explore the representation of music in the novel by first considering its significance to the story – noting its continuing ability to evoke images in modern readers – before examining the uncanny similarities between the music of Orwell's 1984 and the pop music produced today.

MUSIC AS SUBVERSIVE FACTOR IN *NINETEEN EIGHTY-FOUR*

Continuing to resonate with 21st century readers, the music of Orwell's 1984 plays a crucial role in creating what Taylor (op cit) refers to as the 'mental atmosphere' that ultimately leads Winston to the realisation that the future belongs 'to the proles' (1983 [1949]: 206). It begins with the melodic nursery rhyme 'oranges and lemons', a relic of times past, which serves as the symbolic forbidden fruit that first stirs in Winston a sense of primaeval longing. This feeling later intensifies during one of the furtive forays he and Julia make into the land of the lumpen when the 'powerful contralto' of a prole woman hanging clothes wafts like a breeze of humanity through the window of their rented room above Charrington's junk shop:

> It was only an 'opeless fancy,
> It passed like an Ipril dye,
> But a look an' a word an' the dreams they stirred
> They 'ave stolen my 'eart awye! (ibid: 127-128).

As Winston gazes out the window a short while later, the melody once again permeates his consciousness as the woman, knowing 'the whole driveling song by heart', belts out – 'with deep feeling' – another verse:

> They sye that time 'eals all things,
> They sye you can always forget;
> But the smiles an' the tears across the years
> They twist my 'eart-strings yet! (ibid: 131).

Providing the context, the narrator informs us:

> The tune had been haunting London for weeks past. It was one of countless similar songs published for the benefit of the proles by a sub-section of the Music Department. The words of these songs were composed without any human intervention whatever on an instrument known as a versificator. But the woman sang so tunefully as to turn the dreadful rubbish into an *almost* [my emphasis] pleasant sound (ibid: 128).

'Almost' is perhaps an understatement, however, for although Winston himself is not immediately aware of it, the music begins to infuse his soul like a tonic as the woman's voice floats 'upward with the sweet summer air, very tuneful, charged with a sort of happy melancholy', giving one 'the feeling that she would have been perfectly content ... to remain there for a thousand years'[2] (ibid: 131). Winston is struck by the sense of contentedness she exudes, and there is a timeless quality about the way in which she evokes the 'poor but happy' trope, calling to my mind both the Hungarians with the accordion in the Carl Sandburg poem 'Happiness' (of 1916) and the spirited Irish jig done by Jack and Rose in the 3rd class quarters below deck in the 1997 Hollywood blockbuster *Titanic*. It occurs to Winston that 'he had never heard a member of the Party singing alone and spontaneously' as it 'would even have seemed slightly unorthodox, a dangerous eccentricity, like talking to oneself', prompting him to wonder whether 'it was only when people were somewhere near the starvation level that they had anything to sing about' (ibid: 131). While perhaps subconsciously, the woman's singing awakens in Winston a newfound empathy and respect for the proletariat.

The next reference to the tune stands it in contrast to 'the Hate Song', an odious military march, 'which was to be the theme-song of Hate Week'. The narrator tells us: 'It had a savage, barking rhythm which could not exactly be called music, but resembled the beating of a drum. Roared out by hundreds of voices to the tramp of marching feet, it was terrifying' (ibid: 137). This passage, too, is evocative, conjuring in my mind images of the song blasted from speakers mounted on black buses like those used by Japanese ultra-nationalist *uyoku* groups, although in the novel, the song is 'endlessly plugged on the telescreens' (ibid: 137), perhaps more like MTV. 'The proles had taken a fancy to it, and in the midnight streets it competed with the still-popular "It was only a hopeless fancy".' Even the Parsons children know it and 'play it at all hours of the night and day, unbearably, on a comb and a piece of toilet paper' (ibid: 137-138). The full consequence of the passage, however, is not made clear until the final reference to the song, which occurs as Winston and Julia awaken from a nap just before they are arrested, when Winston hears 'the usual deep-lunged singing … from the yard below': the 'driveling song seemed to have kept its popularity' and was 'still heard … all over the place'. Significantly, we are told: 'It had outlived the Hate Song' (ibid: 203-204).

The passage thus suggests that the proles might yet prevail over the Party, foreshadowing an idea that later occurs to Winston. More importantly, although Winston considers the song 'dreadful rubbish', its impact on him is pivotal, for it is the utterly human act of the woman's singing that first attracts his attention and later inspires his deep admiration for the woman and a subconscious longing for the simplicity she represents. In fact, Winston even begins to regard as 'beautiful' (ibid: 204) the woman who had earlier been described as 'monstrous' and 'solid as a Norman pillar' (ibid: 127). Ultimately, it is the song – and this woman's clothes peg rendition of it, in particular – that drives Winston to conclude: 'If there was hope, it lay in the proles!' (ibid: 205). A subversive little ditty, indeed. Clearly, music is an understated, perhaps, yet powerful theme in the novel, and Orwell's rich imagery continues to evoke mental images that evolve with the times.

'A HOPELESS FANCY': A PORTENT OF SONGS TO COME?

Seventy years have now elapsed since the novel was written, including the thirty-five years that have vaporised since the once 'futuristic' year of 1984. In recent years, the music of the novel has taken on a new level of significance, for the music of Orwell's imaginary world of 1984 in many ways parallels the music actually produced today.

CAROL BIEDERSTADT

First of all, similar to Orwell's 'Music Department', which created the songs that were heard 'all over the place' (ibid: 204) and 'endlessly plugged on the telescreens' (ibid: 137), a monopolistic music industry comprised of three huge companies now produces most modern pop hits (McDonald 2018) and, through cooperation with radio stations, controls where and when we hear them.[3] It works like this: music-making is a costly business, and only major labels have the resources needed to produce hits (Seabrook 2015a: 193). These companies invest millions in their songs[4] and then fight to have them heard, particularly in the USA, for as John Seabrook explains: 'Big Radio is still the best way – some would argue, the only way – to create hits' (ibid: 193). 'Payola' has long been a practice in the American music industry, and despite anti-payola legislation dating back to the 1930s (Messitte 2014), the practice of greasing palms in exchange for airplay continues, although the current use of middle-men – independent promoters known as 'Indies'– allows them to legally skirt the rules (Howard 2011).

Thus, operating within the limits of legality, major labels and their independent promoters do whatever it takes to have their songs heard – everywhere (Seabrook op cit: 193). This became easier in 1996 when the removal of regulations regarding the number of radio stations a single company could own enabled a few huge companies to take control of the majority of American radio stations, paving the way for 'homogenized programming and research-driven play lists' across the country (ibid: 77-78; see also *insideradio.com* (2019)). Modern streaming services further contribute to the ubiquity of certain songs. In 2014, for example, it was found that Pandora, entering a deal with Merlin, was '"steering" its algorithms to perform more music from the Merlin catalogue in exchange for lower rates' (Rae 2014). But it gets worse: employing something bordering on doublethink, Seabrook explains that songs do not become hits because we like them; conversely, he says: 'If the song seems to be playing everywhere at the same time, all at once … it is perceived to be a hit, and becomes one' (op cit: 193). This is due to what psychologists have labeled the 'mere exposure effect', which holds that the more familiar something is, the more people tend to like it (Spiegel 2014). Thus, much like in *Nineteen Eighty-Four*, by controlling what we hear and where we hear it, the modern music industry is brainwashing a captive audience into liking its songs. This could certainly be regarded as an Orwellian outcome.

But the similarities don't stop there. Much like the 'countless similar songs' in Orwell's novel, most would agree that much of today's music sounds the same. This is not surprising, as similar to the 'sub-section' of the Music Department that composes all the music in Orwell's novel, the same handful of people in the music industry, most notably, Max Martin and Dr. Luke, (whom Seabrook refers to as 'the Spielbergs and Lucases of our national headphones'), along with their teams of collaborators, have written a disproportionate number of the pop hits of recent years (op cit: 8). Commenting on the prolificacy of Max Martin,[5] who leads this exclusive pack, Vilhelm Carlström points out he 'is at least very close to being the best of all time', closely trailing John Lennon and Paul McCartney for writing credits and The Beatles' producer George Martin for producer credits (2018). Simon Cowell has even gone so far as to liken him unwittingly to Orwell's versificator in saying: 'I don't think that Max Martin is human. ... I think he was made in Sweden to make hit records, because nobody human can have done what he's done' (cited in Savage 2018).

Also contributing to the homogeneity of today's songs is a method through which songwriters further exploit the 'mere exposure effect' by hooking listeners with a string of familiar notes. Patrick Metzger, who labels this progression 'the Millennial Whoop', explains: 'It's a sequence of notes that alternates between the fifth and third notes of a major scale, typically starting on the fifth. ... A singer usually belts these notes with an "Oh" phoneme, often in a "Wa-oh-wa-oh" pattern. And it is in so many pop songs it's criminal' (2016). The effects of this familiar sequence are uncanny:

> . . . the Millennial Whoop evokes a kind of primordial sense that everything will be alright. You know these notes. You've heard this before. There's nothing out of the ordinary or scary here. ... You're safe. In the age of climate change and economic injustice and racial violence, you can take a few moments to forget everything and shout with exuberance at the top of your lungs. Just dance and feel how awesome it is to be alive right now. Wa-oh-wa-oh (ibid).

The Millennial Whoop thus seems to make modern listeners feel much the same way Winston feels when he hears the crooning prole and momentarily forgets that he lives in a totalitarian surveillance state and can be arrested and tortured at any moment. Might the Millennial Whoop, then, have been something else Orwell envisioned?

Had Orwell only extended the application of the versificator to the music and not only the lyrics of the songs of his imaginary future, his predictions would have been almost completely accurate. Still, his vision is not far removed from the modern reality. For sure, the big players in today's music industry are doing their best to reduce the human element and hone hit-making into hard science, and they do this in several seemingly 'Orwellian' ways. Max Martin, for example, uses a method he dubs 'melodic math', which involves fitting 'the syllables to the sounds' regardless of 'whether the resulting lines make sense' (Seabrook 2015b), and one can easily imagine something akin to 'A Hopeless Fancy' being composed in this manner. In addition, while still in need of tweaking, 'Hit Song Science' and similar computer-based technologies have been developed to predict mathematically a song's hit potential (Seabrook 2015a: 144). But technology has also been harnessed in far more questionable ways. Since louder has come to mean better, for example, it is now common practice to make music louder by compressing its dynamic range, even though doing so, as Geoffrey Morrison says, results in a loss of emotion and songs that are 'much more artificial, less like musicians playing music' (2011). Worse still, as drummer and percussionist Greg Ellis explains, a digital metronome known as 'the Click' now emits a 'reference pulse' to which virtually all music is now mechanically synchronised, and in 1986 – fitting almost exactly into Orwell's timeframe – a drum machine using 'digitally recorded samples of actual drums' was introduced. Since then even this has been replaced 'by easier to use pre-recorded samples and loops', largely eliminating the need for drummers in studio recordings (n.d.: 10-11). One can envision something like 'the Click' and drum machines and loops producing the Hate Song's 'savage, barking rhythm which could not exactly be called music, but resembled the beating of a drum' (Orwell op cit: 137).

Scariest of all, however, is the recent trend of manipulating the human voice. As Ellis explains: 'All instruments, including the voice, now live in the computer. Using a digital recording application called "auto tune" a singer's pitch can be tuned digitally so singing on key is no longer necessary' (n.d.: 11). Yet, even this has been stretched to new limits and, instead of being used as solely a 'fix-it-in-the-mix application after the event', it is now used to create a range of vocal effects ranging from the robotic to the otherworldly, and 'some speculate that it features in 99 per cent of today's pop music' (Reynolds 2018). As Simon Reynolds puts it: 'Auto-Tune and other forms of vocal effecting are the primary color in the audio palette of a new psychedelia. Appropriately for these dispiriting and despiritualized times, it's a hollowed-out and decadent update, oriented around razing rather than raising consciousness' (ibid), and it does not get much more Orwellian than that.

CONCLUSION

Music may be only a minor element in Orwell's *Nineteen Eighty-Four*, yet it is one whose significance has kept in step with the times. Not only is it a key element in Winston's epiphany, but it continues to evoke a mental atmosphere that resonates with readers.

Most remarkably, Orwell's depiction of music was in many ways prophetic. In fact, much of his description of the music of the future is so eerily accurate that one would swear he had a third eye. Orwell left us no sheet music to accompany the lyrics the washerwoman sings so powerfully, so we can never know for sure, but somehow I can't help but think he envisioned the tune belted out with a husky contraltified and Auto-Tuned millennial whoop: "But a look an' a word an' the dreams they stirred / They 'ave stolen my 'eart a-WY-ee, WY-ee!"

NOTES

[1] Indeed, music seems so tangential to the story that I was at first surprised to read Anne-Marie Simon-Vandenbergen's claim that *Nineteen Eighty-Four* contains a full 89 references to music, although she admits to defining music in a 'broad sense, including references to "singing", "chanting" and "rhythm"' (1992: 172)

[2] Consider, in contrast, Winston's reaction to the woman 'squalling a patriotic song' on the telescreen: 'Her voice seemed to stick into his brain like jagged splinters of glass' (op cit: 94-95)

[3] The companies are Sony BMG, Universal Music Group (UMG purchased EMI in 2012) and Warner Music Group (McDonald 2018)

[4] Yet even with this massive outlay, it was reported in 2011 that 'approximately 85% of the investments of an average record label are unsuccessful from a financial point of view' (Galuska 2011)

[5] Max Martin has written hits for the Backstreet Boys, 'NSync, Britney Spears, Katy Perry, Taylor Swift, Pink, Maroon 5, Justin Timberlake and Kelly Clarkson (Carlström 2018)

REFERENCES

Carlström, Vilhelm (2018) 'The greatest songwriter of all time' is making a west end musical – here are all of Max Martin's No. 1 hits, *Nordic Business Insider*, 13 August. Available online at https://nordic.businessinsider.com/here-are-all-of-max-martins-no.1-billboard-hits--/, accessed on 11 September 2018

Ellis, Greg (n.d.) The click, unpublished manuscript

Galuska, Patryk (2011) Undisclosed payments to promote records on the radio: An economic analysis of anti-payola legislation, *Virginia Sports and Entertainment Law Journal*, Fall

Howard, George (2011) How to get your song on commercial radio, *TuneCore*, 15 September. Available online at https://www.tunecore.com/blog/2011/09/how-to-get-your-song-on-commercial-radio.html, accessed on 17 September 2018

insideradio.com (2019) Who owns what, *insideradio.com*, 4 February. Available online at http://www.insideradio.com/resources/who_owns_what/, accessed on 6 February 2019

McDonald, Heather (2018) How the big four record labels became the big three, *The Balance*, 16 December. Available online at https://www.thebalancecareers.com/big-three-record-labels-2460743, accessed on 6 January 2019

Messitte, Nick (2014) How payola laws keep independent artists off mainstream radio, *Forbes*, 30 November. Available online at https://www.forbes.com/sites/nickmessitte/2014/11/30/how-payola-laws-keep-independent-artists-off-mainstream-radio/#231e8060519f, accessed on 15 September 2018

Metzger, Patrick (2016) The millennial whoop: A glorious obsession with the melodic alternation between the fifth and the third, *Patterning*, 20 August. Available online at *https://thepatterning.com/2016/08/20/the-millennialwhoop-a-glorious-obsession-with-the-melodic-alternation-between-the-fifth-and-the-third/*, accessed on 7 June 2018

CAROL BIEDERSTADT

Morrison, Geoffrey (2011) Compression is killing your music, *CNET*, 8 July. Available online at https://www.cnet.com/news/compression-is-killing-your-music/, accessed on 15 June 2018

Orwell, George (1983 [1949]) *Nineteen Eighty-Four*, London: Longman

Rae, Casey (2014) Fear and loathing in royalty rate setting, *Future of Music Coalition*, 29 October. Available online at https://futureofmusic.org/blog/2014/10/29/fear-and-loathing-royalty-rate-setting, accessed on 10 December 2018

Reynolds, Simon (2018) How Auto-Tune revolutionized the sound of popular music, *Pitchfork*, 17 September. Available online at https://pitchfork.com/features/article/how-auto-tune-revolutionized-the-sound-of-popular-music/, accessed on 16 February 2019

Savage, Mark (2018) Could Max Martin's musical be the best pop show of all time? *BBC*, 1 August. Available online at https://www.bbc.com/news/entertainment-arts-45030675, accessed on 22 December 2018

Seabrook, John (2015a) *The Song Machine*, New York: W. W. Norton

Seabrook, John (2015b) Blank space: What kind of genius is Max Martin? *New Yorker*, 30 September. Available online at https://www.newyorker.com/culture/cultural-comment/blank-space-what-kind-of-genius-is-max-martin, accessed on 10 December 2018

Simon-Vandenbergen, Anne-Marie (1992) Speech, music and dehumanisation in George Orwell's *Nineteen Eighty-Four:* A linguistic study of metaphors, *Language and Literature*, Vol. 2, No. 3

Spielgel, Alix (2014) Play it again and again, Sam, *NPR*, 7 April. Available online at https://www.npr.org/sections/health-shots/2014/04/07/300178813/play-it-again-and-again-sam, accessed on 20 January 2019

Taylor, D. J. (2005) Big Brother sings, *Independent*. 1 May. Available online at https://www.independent.co.uk/arts-entertainment/music/features/big-brother-sings-491439.html, accessed on 12 November 2018

NOTE ON THE CONTRIBUTOR

Carol Biederstadt is an Assistant Professor in the Humanities Division at Union County College, Cranford, New Jersey, USA.

Child Lore in *Nineteen Eighty-Four*

KRISTIN BLUEMEL

Many of us who grew up during the Cold War first read *Nineteen Eighty-Four* in high school, encountering in its grim mythologies the sources of some of our first grown-up feelings about the adult political world. Now we could see, with new-found Orwellian insight, what had been hidden: a global social foundation built of lies, betrayals and torture. It was a painful awakening, but one that launched some of Orwell's youngest readers into a lifetime of reading and re-reading *Nineteen Eighty-Four*. If they were like me, these readers may have sought in later years for some new sign of hope, some new indicator of social redemption hidden among the proles. Does *Nineteen Eighty-Four* get any more hopeful, any less depressing, for its readers as they grow from children to young adults and from young adults to old adults?

The older I get, the more interested I become in Orwell's treatment of children and children's lore. This interest corresponds to my relatively late adoption in a career of teaching British modernism of children's literature as a formal field of study. I now read Orwell's last great novel for its representations of children, rather than or in addition to reading it for the political energies that galvanised me as a child. One can never leave the politics and pessimism behind, but one can look for alternatives to the seeming totality of cynicism and irony symbolised by the rhymes of 'Under the spreading chestnut tree'. Interestingly, Orwell's version of 'Under the spreading chestnut tree' is described in online cram pages as 'a nursery rhyme of the time Orwell was growing up', which the writers helpfully identify as *The Chestnut Tree* by Glen (sic) Miller 1939'.[1] While Glenn Miller's popular swing tune must, indeed, be seen as one of the auditory allusions Orwell's post-World War II readers would recognise, the rhyme in *Nineteen Eighty-Four* that seems to hold out more opportunity for serious study of an authentic British children's lore is 'Oranges and lemons'. This nursery rhyme is what Orwell's contemporaries, the folklorists Iona and Peter Opie, would call a game rhyme, and for those of you who have not looked it up in a while, here are the words:

KRISTIN BLUEMEL

Oranges and lemons,
Say the bells of St. Clement's.

You owe me five farthings,
Say the bells of St. Martin's.

When will you pay me?
Say the bells at Old Bailey.

When I grow rich,
Say the bells at Shoreditch.

When will that be?
Say the bells of Stepney.

I do not know,
Says the great bell at Bow.

Here comes a candle to light you to bed,
And here comes a chopper to chop off your head!
Chip chop chip chop the last man is dead! (Opie and Opie 1997 [1951]: 337-338).

Charrington is correct when he tells Winston that the rhyme was 'a kind of dance. They held out their arms for you to pass under, and when they came to *Here comes a chopper to chop off your head* they brought their arms down and caught you' (Orwell 2003 [1949]: 101). In *The Oxford Dictionary of Nursery Rhymes*, published one year after Orwell's death, the Opies document historic variations of the song, its possible origins, the identities of the churches, and the multiple meanings of the ominous last two lines whose utterance determined who would be in or out of the children's game. Of course, what is missing from the recitation of the rhyme in *Nineteen Eighty-Four* are children singing it. We hear the words as fragments of remembered verse repeated in the voices of adults. This may be to Orwell's point, but it is not to the Opies'. Again and again, in their numerous collections of British nursery rhymes, children's games and songs, including *The Oxford Nursery Rhyme Book* (1955), *The Lore and Language of School Children* (1959) and *Children's Games in Street and Playground* (1969), the Opies emphasise the autonomous, child-directed, anti-authoritarian, rebellious, 'savage' verses of a traditional children's oral culture that co-existed beside the children's print culture of their own day and Orwell's.

In her introduction to the 1992 reprint edition of *I Saw Esau: The Schoolchild's Pocket Book*, illustrated by Maurice Sendak, Iona Opie recalls that when she and her husband first published the book in 1947, they sought to recognise:

… the particular genus of rhymes that belongs to school children. They were clearly not rhymes that a grandmother might sing to a grandchild on her knee. They have more oomph and zoom; they pack a punch. Many are directly concerned with the exigencies of school life: the need for a stinging reply when verbally attacked; the need for comic complaints in the face of persecution or the grinding drudgery of school work; the need to know some clever rhymes by heart, with which to win popularity. They pass from one child to another without adult interference (Opie, Iona 1992: 11-12).

Thus, in the very year that Orwell was composing a novel that assumes a government monopoly over a mechanised popular oral culture, of – in effect – the Glenn Millerfication of English folk culture and folk song, Iona and Peter Opie were reminding readers that characters like Julia would not, in childhood, have learned 'Oranges and lemons' from a grandfather (Orwell 2003 [1945]: 149). Rather, they were more likely to have learned it from peers. This historic marginalisation of children's verse from mainstream culture suggests a source of hope for Orwell's sorry inhabitants of Airstrip One that exceeds his and most of his readers' imaginations. Children will always sing and play games and versify 'without adult interference'. There's a vernacular oral culture that flourishes ungoverned, disrupting rules and defying detection. This is the culture of the hidden, missing prole children of *Nineteen Eighty-Four*.

In Iona Opie's 2017 obituary in the *Guardian*, she is quoted as having said about herself and her husband: 'We were both puritans; we liked hurting ourselves. … Neither of us liked luxury. I wanted a hard life.' The *Guardian* writer comments: 'She got it' (*Guardian* 2017). Whether the attraction to the hard life was a prerequisite for study of nursery rhymes or whether study of nursery rhymes drew the Opies to hardness, there is no denying the hard violence of many of the verses in the Opies's volumes. The brutal violence reserved for Winston and Julia in Orwell's novel, predicted by Orwell's deployment of a nursery rhyme about citrus fruit and church bells, is playfully anticipated in the centuries-old violent rhymes included in *I Saw Esau*. As Iona Opie points out, such rhymes are 'a declaration of a child's brave defiance in the face of daunting odds' (Opie, Iona 1992: 13). In other words, rather than linked to punishment for defiance of authority, they are the street smart, unauthorised, anarchic texts constituting defiance itself. Children 'can get [their] own back, good-humoredly, with an audacious rhyme' (ibid). When she made this comment, Iona Opie may have had *I Saw Esau's* rhyme number 18 in mind:

When I was a chicken
As big as a hen,

KRISTIN BLUEMEL

> My mother hit me
> And I hit her again;
> My father came in,
> And he ordered me out,
> So I up with my fist
> And I gave him a clout (Opie and Opie 1992: 30).

Elaborating on the way nursery rhymes are fantasies of reversal, in which the smallest humans can become masters of their fates through physical confrontation and even destruction of others, Iona Opie points out that, in rhymes, a child's power 'is so great that he can eat his own mother if need be' (1992: 13-14). With this, she directs readers to Sendak's illustration of rhyme number 85 classified under 'Guile-Malicious'; here we see a page with eight small illustrations showing the progression from a baby boy squalling to the same baby boy taking its mother's breast, to swallowing the breast, then swallowing the mother's head, then all of the mother. The baby emerges in the last frame as a monstrously self-satisfied gluttonous figure in a nightdress, dancing upright on a stool (Opie and Opie 1997 [1951]: 74). The rhyme on the opposing page reads:

> I one my mother.
> I two my mother.
> I three my mother.
> I four my mother.
> I five my mother.
> I six my mother.
> I seven my mother.
> I ate my mother (ibid: 75).

This rhyme seems to speak to Winston's past at least as forcefully as 'Oranges and lemons' speaks to his future. It jubilantly foregrounds the child's murderous urge to self-preservation that also motivated the child Winston's more metaphorical, more tortured consumption of his doomed mother. Winston's childhood consumption of his baby sister is just as vividly and playfully anticipated by rhyme number 81:

> I went to my father's garden,
> And found an Irish farthing.
> I gave it to my mother
> To buy a baby brother.
> My brother was so nasty,
> I baked him in a pasty,
> The pasty wasn't tasty
> So I threw it over the garden wall,
> I threw it over the garden wall.
>   Die once!
>   Die twice!

>   Die three times and never no more,
>   And never – no – more! (ibid: 72).

Iona and Peter Opie help us see the situational logic of this game rhyme, one that was chanted to end a person's turn on a swing. 'After the two big pushes that throw the swinger "over the garden wall", no more pushes are given and the swing is allowed to die down' (Opie and Opie 1997 [1951]: 148). Knowledge of this oral history, knowledge of the way the rhyme was shared among children who were playing rather than plotting the destruction of their kindred, helps us bear up under the very different vision of children's power in *Nineteen Eighty-Four*. It gives us courage to read the novel again.

An in-depth knowledge of British nursery rhymes cannot make *Nineteen Eighty-Four*'s vision of childhood, children, or children's rhymes any less nasty than it ever has been. But the Opies's 'audacious' collections playfully speak back to Orwell's great, grim novel. Iona Opie's *Guardian* obituary is again instructive:

> The Opies applied years of rigour to an oral culture too commonplace to have received attention before: their scholarship, informally communicated, was important to the post-war discovery of the words of ordinary people. 'It took 50 generations to make up Mother Goose,' Iona said. 'Nursery rhymes are the smallest great poems of the world's literature' (*Guardian* 2017).

Here, indeed, is hope for all of us who want more from Orwell's proles than drying diapers and 'It was only an 'opeless fancy' (Orwell op cit: 224-225). Such hope springs from nothing less than the childhood energies distilled into the great commonplace poems, those hundreds of nursery rhymes, game songs and chants that the Opies had the good sense and good fortune to hunt down, collect and record.

NOTE

[1] See 'enotes' https://www.enotes.com/homework-help/quot-under-spreading-chestnut-tree-sold-you-you-21701. See also 'Literary Devices'. Available online at https://literarydevices.net/under-the-spreading-chestnut-tree/

REFERENCES

Guardian (2017) Iona Opie Obituary, 25 October. Available online at https://www.theguardian.com/books/2017/oct/25/iona-opie-obituary

Opie, Iona (1992) Introduction, *I Saw Esau: The Schoolchild's Pocket Book*, Cambridge, MA: Candlewick Press

Opie, Iona and Opie, Peter (eds) (1992) *I Saw Esau: The Schoolchild's Pocket Book*, Cambridge, MA: Candlewick Press

KRISTIN BLUEMEL

Opie, Iona and Opie, Peter (eds) (1997 [1951]) *The Oxford Dictionary of Nursery Rhymes*, Oxford: Oxford University Press, second edition

Orwell, George (2003 [1949]) *Nineteen Eighty-Four*, New York: Plume/Penguin Books

NOTE ON THE CONTRIBUTOR

Kristin Bluemel is Professor of English and Wayne D. McMurray Endowed Chair in the Humanities at Monmouth University. She is author of books and articles on modernist and intermodernist writers, including the monograph *George Orwell and the Radical Eccentrics: Intermodernism in Literary London* (Palgrave 2004). Her work in progress is on the eighteenth-century Newcastle wood engraver, Thomas Bewick, black and white children's book illustration, and the twentieth-century wood engraving revival.

'23-F' vs '24-F': On learning about Orwell at a momentous time in Spanish history

JESÚS ISAÍAS GÓMEZ LÓPEZ

It was 1981 when, as an average high school student in Granada, Spain, I came across the name of George Orwell for the first time. I still remember the vivid image of my teacher of Spanish literature showing us an old copy of *Nineteen Eighty-Four* in Spanish, with creasings on the cover, signs of wear and some markings on the inside as she was flipping through the pages.

I remember it was the first class of that day, which was a Monday, with a whole week of classes ahead of us and plenty of time to investigate such an intriguing author and novel, if needed. The teacher, whose name was Rosarito, an attractive young lady in her late twenties or early thirties, strong and agile, with dark penetrating eyes and thick eyebrows that provided her certain savage charm, had, all of a sudden, decided to change the topic of the day from Camilo José Cela to George Orwell. Instead of the lesson on Cela's novel *La Colmena* (*The Hive*), we received a whole introductory lesson on *Nineteen Eighty-Four* and George Orwell.

The class lasted less than one hour and my classmates and I, who were between 15 and 16-years-old, were so delighted by Rosarito's summary of the plot and the connections she made between the world of the novel and our Spanish society that the time flew by too fast. Why such sudden change of the syllabus of Spanish literature? During the previous evening there had been an attempted coup d'état in Spain, led by Lieutenant Colonel Antonio Tejero. With the passage of time, this deplorable event would be regarded in the country by the numeronym '23-F' (standing for 23 February). My classmates and I were aware of the fact that our Spanish democracy was just six-years-old, and only five years younger than us. And unfortunately, the group of students was divided into two opposing sides, those supporting the coup attempt and those of us who felt great relief when only one hour later we received the news that the coup had failed. Regrettably, our society was still morally fragmented and our young democracy was still a fragile and delicate plant.

JESÚS ISAÍAS GÓMEZ LÓPEZ

I personally received George Orwell, with the naivety of a teenager close to sixteen, as a hero and a saviour who had brought a powerful warning to our political institutions. If '23-F' brings back bleak memories to my mind, the following day, '24-F', conjures up an image of some of the most gratifying and revealing lessons I have ever enjoyed. To me, life is a rare thing, and, at least from my own experience, I am convinced that the best lessons occur by chance but happen for a reason: Tejero, a cold-blooded totalitarian, brought the nightmare of '23-F'; Rosarito, a teacher of Spanish literature, brought us the appeasing '24-F' – with *Nineteen Eighty-Four* and its moral and social teaching to prevent us from repeating the mistakes of the past.

NOTE ON THE CONTRIBUTOR

Jesús Isaías Gómez-López is Associate Professor of English literature and Translation at the Department of Philology at the University of Almería, Spain. He graduated from the University of Granada with a PhD in Philology (1998). Professor Gómez-López has published monographs, editions and articles mainly on James Joyce, Aldous Huxley and George Orwell, among other twentieth-century English and American writers. His most recent monographs include *George Orwell, el último hombre de Europa* (Síntesis, 2018); *Mono y esencia* (annotated translation with introduction of Huxley's *Ape and Essence*, Cátedra 2017); George Orwell, *Poesía completa* (Visor 2017) and *Aldous Huxley, poeta de paraísos perdidos* (Síntesis 2016). He is Director of the Research Group, Lenguaje y Pensamiento: Relaciones de Significación entre el Léxico y Obras Literarias (Language and Thought: Meaning Interrelations between Lexicon and Literary Works). Altogether, he is involved in nearly ten funded individual or collective research projects. Email: jigomez@ual.es.

(CLOSE) ENCOUNTERS WITH GEORGE?

JOHN RODDEN

I

My late father could barely write a short note. Certainly he never read a book in his life. His formal education in County Donegal did not extend much beyond third grade in a two-room schoolhouse. None of that was exceptional in rural Ireland in the early 1930s.

Begorrah and bejesus, then why in heaven did I, as he was on the cusp of turning sixty in 1984, presume to introduce him to George Orwell? Or was it the reverse? Did my genetic father – long before 1984 – inadvertently introduce *me* to my literary father, Orwell? Hard to say: even today, in the era of DNA testing, paternity can be an elusive matter, no?

Let me explain – and conjecture.

II

My title is a question because all I have are questions. Bizarre and wildly improbable as it sounds even to my own ears, did my father ever meet Orwell? Perhaps even see him revising the manuscript destined to become *Nineteen Eighty-Four*? Perhaps even ask him politely: 'How is your writing getting on?'

Did their paths ever cross? In mid-1947, upon returning to Donegal after another stint as an indentured servant on a Northern Irish farm, my father paid his last goodbye and left home for good. (Starting as a fourteen-year-old in 1939 – the third oldest among fifteen children – he had been auctioned at market by his father to the highest bidder in a series of six-month sales). He took the short Belfast ferry across the sea to Scotland and ventured to his cousins in Glasgow, where the pay would be better, even though strict rationing was still in effect. Thousands of boys and girls from Ireland were heading over at the time.

My father was 22-years-old, a big, strapping lad, willing to do anything for a bob or two – or, truth be told, even tuppence or a threepenny bit. Arriving in Glasgow, he soon found boarding in a rooming house near his cousins in South Lanarkshire, part

JOHN RODDEN

of Greater Glasgow. Immediately he looked for work – not on a farmstead but on construction sites. He toiled as a labourer, jobbing on various sites throughout the city and its environs.

III

Christmas Eve, 1947. A car pulls up at Hairmyres Hospital with desperate cargo: a deathly sick fellow who has ridden all the way from the isle of Jura in the Scottish Hebrides. The gaunt figure is admitted to the tuberculosis ward that evening, as his friend explains the details of his collapse to hospital authorities. The patient's name? Eric Blair. (The name means nothing to staff members of Hairmyres, though decades later it will release a documentary film about the seven-month stay of their most famous patient.) His friend, who has been a visiting guest since July at Blair's home on Jura, is Richard Rees. Blair can afford a private room; among the possessions that Rees unloads, the staff note, is a typewriter.

The nurses in the tuberculosis ward regard Eric as a sometimes willful patient who pounds away on his typewriter amid swirls of cigarette smoke in defiance of their orders to relax more and type less. (Eventually, doctors confiscate the typewriter. Oddly enough, he continues without a hospital objection to puff away like a smokestack.) His nurses learn that he is working on a novel. Its title? *The Last Man of Europe*.

Little do they realise – or perhaps even Blair himself at the time – that the *clackety! clack! clack!* of those pounding keys was announcing in advance the birth of one of the century's literary masterworks.

It is commonly believed that Eric Blair – a.k.a. George Orwell – composed *Nineteen Eighty-Four* at his home, Barnhill, on Jura. It is true that he wrote the first draft there, but the strain led to a physical breakdown in November-December 1947. Within weeks he lost 13 kg, whereupon Rees drove furiously to Hairmyres Hospital, which had an available place. He stayed there seven months until July 1948, a period during which he became the first person in Scotland to be treated with streptomycin, an expensive wonder drug in the USA and virtually unobtainable in Britain because of post-war currency restrictions. (Orwell was able to use his American royalties from *Animal Farm* to purchase it.) He suffered severe side-effects from the streptomycin treatment. By late spring, his doctors broke off treatment with the drug – and returned the typewriter. Orwell spent the remainder of his stay writing, strolling the grounds, and playing croquet.

IV

Built in 1904, Hairmyres Hospital expanded throughout World War II and afterwards to handle the influx of military and civilian casualties; by 1940, it had been designated as an emergency medical centre. It expanded from 250 to 400 beds within a few years. The sanatorium also expanded. In 1948, TB was killing someone every two hours in Scotland, which was the country in Europe with the highest incidence of TB during the early post-war years and the only one where TB cases were continuing to rise unchecked.

Situated on a hill on the edge of East Kilbride, a hamlet of 900 inhabitants before the war, the hospital lies a half-dozen kilometres from the southeast corner of Glasgow. East Kilbride was undergoing its own construction boom by 1947-1948. Because Glasgow had suffered severe housing shortages from bomb damage and an influx of returning war veterans, Britain had begun to build satellite settlements, the so-called New Towns, which were aimed to address the housing crisis. In May 1947, about the time of my father's arrival, the area around the village and hospital were designated as Scotland's first New Town. ('Kilbride' takes its name from Ireland's St. Brigid – often called 'Brid' or 'Bride'– who founded a monastery for nuns and monks in County Kildare in the sixth century A.D.)

My father would have heard about the town from his cousins; St. Brigid is revered in Donegal. How well I remember, during family visits back to Donegal during my own youth, the sight of St. Brigid crosses made of thatch affixed to every doorway and wall in my father's old home – a tradition that my mother continued wherever we lived in the States.

V

As my mind's eye surveys the scene, I wonder: might my father have been hired to work at Hairmyres Hospital when it was undergoing its vast post-war expansion, when the number of beds increased to handle the returning wounded soldiers? Did he and his Glaswegian cousins ride out on their bicycles for Sunday mass, and then stay to walk the hospital grounds, which were favourite strolls for residents and visitors?

He often talked about his work on different sites in Glasgow. He was grateful that he arrived just as double summertime was ending, when work until 10 p.m. was common. I wish I'd thought to ask him specifically about Hairmyres; now it's too late.

If he worked on the construction expansion of the hospital, laboured on the New Town project, or just spent a Sunday afternoon on hospital grounds, he may have spotted a tall, gaunt patient on a spring or summer day. Blair was often walking the grounds or even playing croquet. (Along with 'collapse therapy', which sought to keep the lung disabled and presumably at rest, fresh air and sunshine were the main treatment protocols for TB in the 1940s.) Indeed, a hospital photograph from 1948 depicts a bucolic scene, with a scarecrow figure seated high up in the distance, looking

JOHN RODDEN

out from the veranda. Is it too fanciful to imagine that this may be Blair? And that, on such a day as this, my own father may have glimpsed him there?

As for a visit to East Kilbride, I can well imagine my father and his friends biking out from Busby or taking a bus along the old A726 road one Sunday morning. He was a faithful churchgoer throughout his life, an altar boy in school and as a young man.

In the quite unlikely event that Orwell and my father ever met in the hospital or on the grounds during their months together in South Lanarkshire in 1947-1948, I like to imagine that the fleeting interaction would have been quite cordial. Might my father have seen the emaciated figure hunched over in his lawn chair, scribbling on a sheaf of papers? Perhaps even retrieve a sheet blown away in a gust of wind? And even asked, on returning it, about the grand stack of papers?

My father was a working-class fellow not so different from the miners and labourers whom Orwell visited in Wigan. And not so unlike young English comrades at the Catalonia front such as the 18-year-old Stafford Cottman, who became a lifelong friend of Orwell. For his part, I'm sure that my father would have respected an older, well-spoken, 'elderly' English gentleman with an upper-class Etonian accent. My father never expressed any animosity toward the English; the pay, he said, was better there than in Scotland and Wales – though it was even better, he added quickly, in America.

VI

In 1948, my father and George Orwell parted ways. On leaving Hairmyres in the summer, Orwell returned to Jura and completed his novel by the year's end – and changed its title to *Nineteen Eighty-Four*. Meanwhile, my father headed to Coventry, tipped off by some mates that the bombed-out town offered plenty of work and better pay.

They would meet again, as it were, thirty-five years later – in America, of all places. Back home during a holiday from my PhD studies, I show my father a copy of the new Signet *1984*, introduced by famed TV anchorman Walter Cronkite. Although my father does not recognise the author's name, he faithfully tunes in every evening to Cronkite's news broadcasts.

One evening, my father watches the CBS-TV special, *1984 Revisited*, narrated by Cronkite. 'I just saw Walter Cronkite devote an entire hour to "yer man",' my father tells me excitedly in a telephone call after the telecast (which I have not seen). 'Yer man Orwell must be an important guy!'

My father never went on to read *Nineteen Eighty-Four*. But for years thereafter, he would ask me about 'yer man Orwell', that English writer whom Walter Cronkite so highly esteemed.

NOTE ON THE CONTRIBUTOR

John Rodden is the author of several books about George Orwell including *The Politics of Literary Reputation*, Oxford University Press (1989) and, most recently, *Becoming George Orwell: Life, Literature, Legend, Legacy*, Princeton University Press (2019).

Patriarchal Norms and Sexual Desire in Michael Radford's Film of *Nineteen Eighty-Four*

MARTIN STOLLERY

A confession: I cannot recall when I first read *Nineteen Eighty-Four*. A doubleplusungood admission: I cannot even be sure if I had read the entire book until I was invited to contribute to this dossier. Yet I have always felt I knew it well. My first encounter with the novel is hazy because I came of age when *Nineteen Eighty-Four* was already part of our common culture. My perception of the novel is also filtered through a more vivid recollection of the *1984* film version which I saw when it was first released, aged eighteen, soon after starting a literature and film degree course. For this reason, regardless of critical evaluation, the film is my *Nineteen Eighty-Four*.

The film was screened again at nearly two hundred venues, on 4 April 2017, the date Winston starts writing his diary in 1984, in protest against the Trump administration's attempt to remove National Endowment for the Arts (NEA) funding. This revival also served as a tribute to John Hurt (Winston Smith in the film), who died in January 2017. Similarly, the film featured the last role played by Richard Burton (O'Brien), who died in August 1984. Many commentators have rightly praised these impressive performances. But given that I first saw the film when second wave and, indeed, radical feminism was a significant cultural force at the British university I attended in the mid-1980s, and given the mainstreaming during the Trump era of what some commentators call 'fourth wave feminism', now seems a good time to consider the film's representation of Julia, played by Suzanna Hamilton.

Daphne Patai memorably argued that 'the romance between Julia and Winston is far less important in the novel ... than the 'romance' between Winston and O'Brien' (1984: 239). It provides a different perspective on the *1984* film, in which the stars are Hurt and Burton, not Hamilton. In the opening sequence, Julia and O'Brien are connected through a lengthy panning shot across the crowd indulging in the Two Minutes Hate. This shot starts with Julia on the right edge of the frame and ends with O'Brien centrally framed. This prefigures later moments in the film when Julia and O'Brien switch places in Winston's consciousness. In the next part of the opening sequence, Julia jumps up and throws something at Goldstein's image after it appears on the telescreen. When she sits back down, O'Brien is revealed in the background of the shot, turning to look in her direction. The next shot is a close up of Winston looking left, potentially meeting O'Brien's gaze. The third shot in this series is from the same position as the first, with O'Brien looking away, the hint of a cryptic smile on his face. At the very beginning of the film, Winston seeks recognition from O'Brien's 'marble' eyes (Burton's description, quoted in Ryan 2018: 146), and Julia is a conduit for this exchange of looks between the men.

The 1984 film adaptation changes aspects of the meeting between Winston and O'Brien in the latter's office. In the novel, Winston declares his willingness during this meeting to commit heinous acts for the resistance, such as throwing sulphuric acid in children's faces. In the film, the scene is shortened and this dialogue, that may make us less sympathetic towards Winston, is removed. Julia is also not present. Hamilton has described the film's Julia and her performance as 'very vital' and 'modernised' (quoted in Ryan op cit: 138). Linked to this, director and scriptwriter Michael Radford has explained that he excised Julia from this scene because he viewed her as someone with 'a real strength of her own', who would see no need to 'trail along behind' Winston to O'Brien's office to say virtually nothing (as is the case in the novel) (quoted in ibid: 137). We can assess this change negatively or positively, as accentuating what Patai refers to as the novel's tendency to contrast Julia's 'lack of seriousness with Winston's heroic attempt to understand his society' (op cit: 243), or as throwing into sharper relief what Thomas Horan describes as Julia's 'pragmatic wisdom that is far more valuable than Winston's intellectual theorizing' (2018: 160).

One incident in the *1984* film but not in the novel is O'Brien telling Winston, during his interrogation, that photographs of him and Julia having sex will be 'recycled for proletarian use'. It's a line which can also be understood as a wry, self-reflexive comment, intentional or not, on an element within the film but not the novel. One of the film's selling-points – given that star names, outstanding production design and Orwell's canonical status might not suffice to attract a large enough audience for a grim dystopian narrative – is its sex scenes and Hamilton's full frontal nudity, compared to less frequent, more discreet shots of a naked Hurt. In this respect, the *1984* film builds upon the long history of broadening the appeal of art cinema by pushing boundaries in the representation of sex.

Virgin Films, the financiers, in what was primarily a commercial rather than aesthetic move, commissioned the Eurythmics to produce a pop soundtrack album that orientated the film more towards the youth market. This aggrieved Radford, who preferred a classical instrumental score composed by Dominic Muldowney. The first Eurythmics single from the album, *Sexcrime*, featured in trailers, left no doubt that the film would represent more explicitly than previous adaptations the physical aspects of Winston's and Julia's relationship. The music video, intended for MTV rotation, likewise included shots from the film of Hurt and Hamilton naked. Yet the Eurythmics belonged to a wave of 1980s British pop music characterised by fluid, playful representations of gender and sexuality. Singer Annie Lennox was known for her androgynous style and caused a minor stir at the February 1984 Grammy awards when she performed in Elvis drag.

Any discussion of the *1984* film needs to take these media paratexts into account when considering whether it reinforces patriarchal norms or valorises 'the hunger for self-determination, the ability to empathize and bond with others, and the impetus for moral renewal in sexual desire' which Horan sees as a life-affirming constant in twentieth century dystopian fiction (op cit: 206).

REFERENCES

Horan, Thomas (2018) *Desire and Empathy in Twentieth-Century Dystopian Fiction*, Basingstoke: Palgrave Macmillan

Patai, Daphne (1984) *The Orwell Mystique: A Study in Male Ideology*, Cambridge, Massachusetts: University of Massachusetts Press

Ryan, David (2018) *George Orwell on Screen: Adaptations, Documentaries and Docudramas on Film and Television*, Jefferson, North Carolina: McFarland

NOTE ON THE CONTRIBUTOR

Martin Stollery is an independent researcher and film historian whose books include *Alternative Empires: European Modernist Cinemas and Cultures of Imperialism* (2000) and the co-authored *British Film Editors* (2004). His numerous essays on film history include Orwell as Social Patriot – and British Cinema Studies, in *George Orwell Studies*, Vol. 3, No. 1, 2018.

Who was Julia? – *Nineteen Eighty-Four*'s Many Heroines

D. J. TAYLOR

Critical orthodoxy usually insists that Julia in *Nineteen Eighty-Four* can be identified with Orwell's second wife, Sonia Brownell, whom he married by special licence in his room at University College, London, shortly before his death. A key piece of evidence in this argument is the very first letter that Orwell despatched from the remote Scottish island of Jura in April 1947 on the day after his arrival there to restart work on what became the novel's initial draft (Davison 1998a, Vol. 19: 122-124).

The recipient of this effusion – three pages long and containing minutely itemised instructions on how to reach the island from the mainland ('Travel by bus to West Tarbert ... Take hired car to Lealt...') – was at this point in her career an assistant on Cyril Connolly's literary magazine *Horizon*, where she combined a profound reverence for its editor's intellect with an undisguised desire to take on more of the editorial duties herself. She was also one of the women to whom, in the winter of 1945-1946, traumatised by the death of his first wife Eileen, Orwell had proposed marriage and by whom he had been turned down. A year later, their relationship had progressed to the point where Orwell is anxious to write to her even before his luggage has been unpacked ('Dearest Sonia, I am handwriting this because my typewriter is downstairs'), thank her for purchases made on his behalf ('I've just remembered I never paid you for that brandy you got for me...') and entreat her to visit him ('I want to give you the complete details about the journey, which isn't so formidable as it looks on paper.') Clearly the man who signs off 'with much love', having remarked that 'I do so want to have you here', is desperate to have her by his side (ibid).

Sonia never made it to Jura in Orwell's lifetime. Possibly she was put off by the prospect of a journey so torturous that it took Orwell two dozen lines to describe. Nonetheless, the memory of her, and the time they had spent together in London, would have been at the forefront of his mind as he sat down to recommence work on *Nineteen Eighty-Four* and continue to sketch out the doomed love affair that lies at its core. All this, naturally, encourages a suspicion that Sonia bears some relation to Julia, the 'girl from the Fiction Department', who spends her working hours in a government department engaged on the task of mass-producing pornography for impressionable proles and her leisure hours encouraging Winston to break almost every proscription in the Party rule-book. Hilary Spurling goes even further and declares that Orwell's aim was to 'recreate' Sonia as Julia and 'take her as his model' (Spurling 2002: 67). First catching sight of her as she enters a room in which the Two Minutes Hate is being staged, Winston sees:

> … a bold-looking girl of about twenty-seven, with thick dark hair, a freckled face and swift, athletic movements. A narrow scarlet sash, emblem of the Junior Anti-Sex League, was wound several times round the waist of her overalls, just tightly enough to bring out the shapeliness of her hips (Orwell 2000 [1949]: 12).

Julia's age is later given as 26 (Sonia, by the time Orwell invited to Jura, was in sight of her 29th birthday), and several pointed distinctions are made between her youthful zest and Winston's premature decay: 'I'm thirty-nine-years old. I've got a wife I can't get rid of. I've got varicose veins. I've got five false teeth' (ibid: 138). Orwell, at the time he first asked Sonia to marry him, was in his early forties. In both cases a distinctly unhealthy middle-aged man is obsessed with an energetic woman in her twenties.

After this, though, evidence for the Sonia/Julia identification is much more ambiguous. Winston at one point notes of Julia that 'Except for her mouth, you could not have called her beautiful' (ibid: 145); Sonia, with her ash-blonde hair, pale complexion and slight tendency to plumpness, was thought by her admirers to resemble a Renoir portrait. Like Sonia, Julia has a forceful presence, is said to 'burst' into rooms and has a self-confident vocal style that approaches the bossiness Sonia was thought to bring to her editorial work duties in the *Horizon* office. Julia's declaration that 'I do voluntary work three days a week for the Junior Anti-Sex League. Hours and hours I've spent pasting their bloody rot all over London. I always carry one end of the banner in the processions. I always look cheerful and I never shirk anything' (ibid: 140) sounds very like some of Sonia's quoted remarks. Unlike her supposed model, she is resolutely unintellectual, doesn't care much for reading – to Sonia, the writer David Plante once recalled, 'man could do nothing greater than to write books' (1983) – and falls asleep while Winston regales her with selections from Oceania's legendary banned book, Emmanuel Goldstein's *The Theory and Practice of Oligarchic Collectivism* (Orwell 2000 [1949]: 247).

But there are other pieces of evidence, both from *Nineteen Eighty-Four* and the circumstances of Orwell's own life, which might call the identification into question. To begin with, Orwell had started thinking about the novel well before he became involved with Sonia in the early part of 1946: the first few pages had been written as long ago as the summer of 1945 and the notes in which he sketched out its preliminary outlines may date from as early as 1943. Equally, he had asked several other women to marry him in the aftermath of Eileen's death: there is no guarantee that Sonia stood at the head of the queue. Neither is there any real evidence as to the true state of Orwell and Sonia's relationship in early 1947. Again, critical orthodoxy insists that they had had a brief, and to Sonia, distasteful affair the previous spring, but Sonia's close friend Janetta Parlade (not always a reliable witness) maintained that their solitary sexual encounter came much later, during Orwell's time in the Cranham sanatorium (Parlade n.d.).

Yet other pieces of detail suggest that in *Nineteen Eighty-Four's* central relationship, Orwell was recalling memories of several different women. The *plein air* frolics that Winston enjoys with Julia are prefigured as early as his relationship with Eleanor Jaques, most of which was conducted in the Suffolk verdure in the early 1930s. A letter to Eleanor from September 1932, which recalls 'that day in the wood along past Blythburgh Lodge … I shall always remember that, & your nice white body in the dark moss' is remarkably close to the account of Julia tearing off her clothes so that her body 'gleamed white in the sun' (Davison 1998b: 269). As for Julia's 'swift, athletic movements', it is worth pointing out that Brenda Salkeld, another of Orwell's Suffolk loves from the early 1930s, held down a day-job as gym mistress at a local girls' private school. There is even a suspicion, as W. J. West argues, that Julia's physical appearance owes something to the similarly be-overalled and sash-clad female character in Inez Holden's novel *Night Shift* (1941). Holden knew Orwell for the best part of a decade, visited him on Jura and, to West, 'is in some sense a model for Julia' (West 1992: 189).

A third objection is perhaps more integral to the role that Julia plays in the book, which is to a certain extent figurative rather than decisive. Curiously, with the exception of Winston's opening remarks and one or more speculations about her interior life ('She was very young, he thought, she still expected something from life … She would not accept it as a law of nature that the individual is always defeated … She did not understand that there was no such thing as happiness, that the only victory lay in the far future, long after you were dead' (Orwell 2000 [1949]: 155-156)) we learn very little about Julia, and what goes on in her mind. Winston, with the memory of his miserable, sex-loathing wife to goad him, may find her irresistible, but there is a way in which her importance rests on what she symbolises – youth, impulse, free-spiritedness – rather than what she actually is.

D. J. TAYLOR

But to Spurling, Sonia is not merely transposed on to the pages of *Nineteen Eighty-Four*, she is also a significant influence on its intellectual framework. One of the key concepts of Oceania's totalitarian regime is the state of mind encapsulated by the Newspeak word 'doublethink' – the ability to hold simultaneously in your head two contradictory opinions. There are certainly echoes, or rather foreshadowings, of doublethink in a review Sonia contributed to *Horizon* in July 1946 of *Les Amitiés particulières* by the French writer Roger Peyrefitte. Like the two boys who are its central characters, Sonia had been educated at a Catholic boarding school, and the book reawakened many a hostile memory of the atmosphere of treachery and duplicitousness which she imagined to lie at Catholicism's heart:

> When you have seen through [this] world you can never become its victim, but can fight it with the only unanswerable weapon – cynical despair; when you have learned the lesson of the double visions, action and emotion are equally meaningless. This is the heritage of Catholic education … one which those who went to Catholic schools always recognise in each other, members of a secret society who, when they meet, huddle together, temporarily at truce with the rest of the world, while they, cautiously, untrustingly, lick each other's wounds (Spurling 2002: 69).

It is not known whether this particular issue of *Horizon* reached Jura in the summer of 1946, but Spurling thinks it 'hard to write off as coincidence the fact that, at the very moment when he started work on *Nineteen Eighty-Four*, his ex-mistress outlined in print precisely the scenario that would become the central section of his plot' (ibid: 68). On the other hand, a trawl through Orwell's journalism suggests that he had been attempting to equate religious faith with left- and right-wing forms of autocracy throughout the early 1940s. There is, for example, an unpublished review originally filed for the *Manchester Evening News* – as with *Animal Farm*, Orwell assumed that it was rejected for its 'anti-Stalin implications' – of Harold Laski's *Faith, Reason and Civilisation*. (Davison 1998c: 122-125). Laski's aim was to square his belief in democracy and freedom of thought with his conviction that the Soviet Union was 'the real dynamo of the Socialist movement in this country and everywhere else'. According to Orwell's reading, Laski does this by drawing an analogy between the USSR and Christianity in the period of the break-up of the Roman Empire; Soviet socialism 'aims at the establishment of human brotherhood and equality just as single-mindedly as the early church aimed at the establishment of the Kingdom of God' (ibid).

Certainly, there are traces of Sonia in *Nineteen Eighty-Four*, just as there are hints of Eileen, who in her late twenties contributed a three-part futurist satire entitled 'End of the Century: 1984' to her old school magazine, which Orwell is highly likely to have seen (Taylor 2003: 375). Meanwhile, there is a final reason for wondering whether the girl in the Fiction Department is a straightforward projection of the girl who fussed over Cyril Connolly in the *Horizon* office. This is the question of Julia's motivation, and the ultimate value of her feelings for Winston. For O'Brien, the potentate of the Inner Party, the sacerdotal, schoolmasterly figure who encourages Winston in his rebellion, is eventually revealed as an agent provocateur; the plot is a put-up job; there is at least a suspicion that Julia is O'Brien's willing accomplice, the honey-trap expressly set in place with the aim of luring Winston into danger and throwing him into the hands of the Thought Police. *Nineteen Eighty-Four* may well, from one angle, be a love-letter from Jura to a girl left behind in London. From another, its central message is horribly unromantic, nothing less than an insistence that in the end the people we love are guaranteed to betray us.

REFERENCES

Davison, Peter (ed.) (1998a) *Orwell: The Complete Works*, Vol. 19, London, Secker & Warburg

Davison, Peter (ed.) (1998b) *Orwell: The Complete Works*, Vol. 10, London, Secker & Warburg

Davison, Peter (ed.) (1998c) *Orwell: The Complete Works*, Vol. 16, London, Secker & Warburg

Orwell, George (2000 [1949]) *Nineteen Eighty-Four*, London and New York: Penguin Books

Parlade, Janetta, unpublished memoir

Plante, David (1983) *Difficult Women: A Memoir of Three*, London: Gollancz

Spurling, Hilary (2002) *The Girl From the Fiction Department: A Portrait of Sonia Orwell*, London: Hamish Hamilton

Taylor, D. J. (2003) *Orwell: The Life*, London: Chatto & Windus

West, W. J. (1992) *The Larger Evils*, Edinburgh: Canongate

NOTE ON THE CONTRIBUTOR

D. J. Taylor's *On* Nineteen Eighty-Four*: A Biography* will be published later this year, as will his *Lost Girls: Love, War and Literature 1939-1951*.

ARTICLES

Names in *Burmese Days*:
A Fantasia

DOUGLAS KERR

Something odd seems to be going on with names in Orwell's novel of 1934, Burmese Days, *according to Douglas Kerr. They tend to settle into disconcerting pairs. Then, right at the end, the Anglican padre who comes to hold a service at Kyauktada is given no name. How strange. But, through an ingenious process of deduction, Kerr offers here a solution to the Mystery of the Padre with no Name.*

In the novel *Burmese Days*, the central character, John Flory, has a faithful dog named Flo. We are not told whether Flory acquired the dog and named her, or if he inherited her already named. It seems, in any case, an odd coincidence. There is nothing wrong with the name Flo for a dog. But whether or not Flory did, indeed, give the dog her name, he could not have failed to be struck by its closeness to his own. It is rather as if a man called Butcher had a dog called Butch.

Flo could be an abbreviation of Flory or a nickname. There is a nominal identification between master and hound. (And not merely nominal: in one of his bouts of self-disgust, Flory accuses himself of being a 'spineless cur' (1989 [1934]: 62).) It seems appropriate, then, that when Flory is preparing to commit suicide at the end of the story, he takes care to dispose of his four-legged quasi-namesake by blowing her brains out, before serving a similar quittance on himself.

Certain names in *Burmese Days* seem to go together. What follows is a not entirely solemn development of this observation.

Burmese Days is a novel thoroughly obsessed with animals, of course (see Kerr 1999). But there seems to be something odd going on with its names too. They settle into disconcerting pairs. The first syllable of Flory becomes the name of the dog. This seems fair enough; the two are always together, the dog ambling after the man. (But shouldn't she precede him, like a prefix? She precedes him into death at any rate.) Other nominal pairings are more mysterious. Verrall, the military policeman, and Veraswami, the doctor, embark upon the world of the story with the same three literal footsteps. Yet they seem, if anything, opposites, the strutting English narcissist and the kindly if naïve Indian, the one Flory's love rival and the other his only friend. It seems a cynical stroke of fate, or a sardonic stroke of the author's pen, that has gifted them with this odd surnominal proximity.

And what about Elizabeth, the husband-hunting English girl with whom Flory falls in love, and Ellis, the manager of a timber company who is Flory's adversary in the debate about allowing a 'native' member into the European Club. In what sense might Ellis be a contraction of Elizabeth, or Elizabeth an extension of Ellis? Is this a subtextual hint, a secret signal, that it is all too easy to believe that in time Elizabeth might grow (or shrink) into a person like Ellis, her casual anti-Burmese racism metastasising into the full-blown, venomous, sadistic version practised by Ellis?

Yet Ellis is not a natural partner for Elizabeth in the story. Unexpectedly, she will end up with Macgregor, the Deputy Commissioner, marrying him in the final chapter so that – in the cynical last words of the novel – 'she fills with complete success the position for which nature had designed her from the first, that of a *burra* memsahib' (ibid: 300). Macgregor – boring, mediocre, but not unkind – seems more than Elizabeth deserves, and the two of them preside over the end of the story like those improbable partnerships that provide the nucleus for the ending of Shakespeare's *Twelfth Night* – Macgregor a pompous Orsino wed to Elizabeth's empty-headed Viola.

ARTICLE

Meanwhile, the lack of connection between the names of Elizabeth and Macgregor seems to suggest that, at least in the mind of the perverse demon who has charge of naming in this novel, this is not a marriage made in heaven. If Elizabeth is kin to Ellis, then who, according to the secret logic of the novel's nomenclature, is Macgregor's natural partner? Cast your eye down (or up) an imaginary alphabetical index of the characters of *Burmese Days*, and nestling up to Macgregor is Ma Hla May. This is the most scandalous pairing yet. Flory's Burmese mistress, Ma Hla May, is scheming, selfish, meretricious and vindictive: in most obvious ways the opposite of the bumbling but usually harmless Macgregor.

But the pairing of names may be pointing us towards an uncomfortable truth that the novel does not shirk. Ma Hla May is no conventional girlfriend. She is actually a slave. Her parents sold her to Flory for three hundred rupees as a sex object. When he abandons her for Elizabeth, she has nowhere to go, being alienated from her own people and no longer marriageable. She ends up in a brothel in Rangoon. In some ways Ma Hla May is the properly tragic victim of the story, collateral damage in the economic and social impact of invasion and colonisation on a traditional society. Who is responsible for her fate? Well, Flory, obviously. But in a wider sense she is a casualty of empire itself, and the senior officer of that empire in this story is Macgregor. So perhaps there is some justice in his being unwittingly chained to her by the front of his name.

After this, we have to reach a bit further to find other name pairings. A case might just about be made for a name kinship between Lackersteen, the alcoholic would-be philanderer who is Elizabeth's uncle, and Li Yeik, the opium-smoking Chinese grocer. One main character, however, seems to have been left on the shelf, without a partner in this nomenclatural dance. This is the magnificent villain, the magistrate U Po Kyin. (The 'U' is an honorific, something between 'Esq' and 'Sir'. Kyin, like the last term in Aung San Suu Kyi's name, begins with a 'ch' sound, so Po Kyin is pronounced 'poe-cheen'.) Besides being a corrupt schemer, the magistrate is an impeccably pious Buddhist. Can we not find a suitable name-partner, indicating a coded kinship, for Po Kyin?

I think I have found an answer in the closing chapters, in the Anglican padre who comes to hold a service at Kyauktada, and stays long enough to preside at Flory's funeral. He is a Dickensian figure, tall, with grey hair and a refined, discoloured face; he wears a pince-nez and preaches interminable sermons (ibid: 281). Unaccountably, Orwell neglected to give him a name. But we can repair that omission, using the principles of naming uncovered here, and speculating that his secret name partner is the pious Buddhist hypocrite, Po Kyin. Obviously, the clergyman must be the Reverend Mr Pigeon.

REFERENCES

Kerr, Douglas (1999) Orwell, animals and the East, *Essays in Criticism*, Vol. 49, No. 3 pp 234-255

Orwell, George (1989 [1934]) *Burmese Days*, London: Penguin

NOTE ON THE CONTRIBUTOR

Douglas Kerr is Honorary Professor of English at the University of Hong Kong and Honorary Research Fellow at Birkbeck College, University of London. He is the author of *George Orwell* in the 'Writers and their Work' series (Northcote House, 2003). His other books are *Wilfred Owen's Voices* (Clarendon Press of Oxford University Press, 1993), *A Century of Travels in China* (co-edited, Hong Kong University Press, 2007), *Eastern Figures: Orient and Empire in British Writing* (Hong Kong University Press, 2008) and *Conan Doyle: Writing, Profession, and Practice* (Oxford University Press, 2013). His main current research interest is in Orwell and Asia.

Orwell and Captain Robinson's 'Poet': A More Than Cautionary Note

PHIL BAKER

It has been argued that 'the Poet', a character in the autobiography of his sometime friend Captain Herbert Reginald Robinson, is actually George Orwell. But, according to Phil Baker, this identification is questionable. It is also possible that Robinson's book has elements of fiction.

During Orwell's time in Burma, where he served in the Indian Imperial Police from 1922 to 1927, we know he was a friend of Captain Herbert Reginald Robinson, described by Orwell biographer Michael Shelden as 'the most disreputable Englishman in Mandalay' (Shelden 1991: 97). Robinson, who features in Darcy Moore's recent paper about Orwell and opium (Moore 2018), was an Indian army officer who transferred to the Burmese Police as an administrator and magistrate. He then turned to opium smoking, spent time as a Buddhist monk, and finally became a rock-bottom opium addict, attempting suicide in 1925.

Robinson's 1942 autobiography, *A Modern De Quincey*, mentions two unidentified friends named only as 'the Poet' and 'the Padre'. It was reviewed by Orwell in the *Observer* ('Portrait of an Addict', 13 September 1942), where he makes it clear he had known Robinson. More recently, Gerry Abbott has suggested (Abbott 2004 and 2006) that Orwell is, in fact, 'the Poet' of Robinson's book.

It is this identification that I would like to consider in more detail. The evidence to be weighed begins with the fact that Orwell did, indeed, write poetry (although this was true of many young men with literary leanings, including Robinson himself). Poetry was important to him, and writing it was a part of his young identity long before he wrote novels. Orwell's poetry is likeable without being particularly distinguished; it is traditional, robust, and tends towards humour, satire and parody, along with romantic love and patriotic decency (Venables 2015). As for Robinson's 'poet', he 'looked what he was – a poet', because he is 'pale and delicate', and as a poet he has 'peculiar fancies', with the capriciousness of a pregnant woman (Robinson 1942: 115). The suggestion seems to be that he is a poet of the more aesthetic variety. This does not sound particularly like Orwell, but Robinson may have slanted his description for comic effect; the inspiration from his friend Orwell might still be there.

Trying to break his opium habit, and contemplating the horrors of withdrawal on an imminent voyage to England, Robinson took advice from a doctor and resorted to the more convenient and medicalised method of injecting morphine. It is with this state of affairs, *en route* to the ship for England, that in or very shortly before June 1924 he puts up at the house of 'the Poet' in Rangoon, where his aunt gives him a shot of morphine. Robinson mentions the aunt in passing as 'a lady whom I dearly loved' (and this is not, in context, about the fact that she injected him), suggesting some prior acquaintance (ibid: 118). The Rangoon connection of 'the Poet' is mentioned once more when in March 1925, shortly before his suicide attempt, Robinson plans to go to Rangoon and find outdoor work with the help of a relation of 'the Poet' (ibid: 138).

Orwell did have family connections to Burma, or certainly gave his choice of Burma as his police posting with the words 'Have had relations there' (Meyers 1972: 52). His mother, Ida Limouzin, had grown up in Moulmein, around 180 miles from Rangoon, and – tantalisingly for Abbott's theory – she had six sisters; at least one aunt, Nora, was still in Burma at Moulmein. But I am so far unable to match Orwell with having a Rangoon house, or an aunt there. At this time, after four months in Myaungma from January 1924, Orwell had just been posted to Twante, a township in the bleak delta region (and in December he moved to Syriam, which is closer to Rangoon – but this is later than Robinson's visit). Twante is about twenty miles from Rangoon, on the other side of the river, and less than two hours away. Jeffrey Meyers's 'ten minutes', correcting D. J. Taylor's slip of 'thirty-six hours' (2003: 69), seems optimistic (Meyers 2010: 214). Perceptions of place and distance are subjective; if I was living in Scotland, would I refer to staying with a friend in Windsor as staying in London? Perhaps. So the identification of Orwell with a Rangoon house and aunt known to Robinson is possible but currently inconclusive.

To return to the question of physical appearance, Orwell at 19 was 'sallow-faced, tall, thin and gangling' (Stansky and Abrahams, cited in Abbott 2006: 46) while 'the Poet' was 'pale and delicate' and 'slight' (Robinson, cited in Abbott 2006: 46). These do not altogether agree. Robinson's description of 'the Poet' conjures up a character who is somewhat effete and 'weedy', whereas Orwell was 6'3", and gangling does not necessarily mean weedy – you can be gangling in a lanky, raw-boned way. As for sallow, it does not mean pale, but yellowish. So despite being 'thin', Orwell seems to have been tall, a little jaundiced-looking (perhaps compounded by a tan), and as far as we know reasonably fit; he was certainly fit enough for police work, and doesn't seem to have been particularly 'delicate'. Significantly, D. J. Taylor, reviewing the second edition of Robinson's book in the *Times Literary Supplement*, disagreed with the identification of Orwell and 'the Poet' on the grounds of Orwell's imposing height (Taylor 2004).

The identification becomes more interesting, and has more at stake, when Robinson's 'Poet' goes elephant shooting; an incident that Abbott mentions, but slides over rather briefly. There is an obvious and immediate association here, at least verbal, with Orwell's 1936 essay 'Shooting an Elephant', but it may be misleading: 'the Poet' has a keen desire to shoot an elephant. Abbott notes (2006: 46) that Orwell was prepared to go tiger shooting with his friend Beadon and was, therefore, not opposed to big game hunting (he was also a keen shot with a .22 in his teens), and this is true, although the savagely predatory nature of the tiger makes it a more dignified and even useful activity. Tiger-shooting – like pig-sticking – was also a far more stereotypical part of the British imperial experience and a mainstay of boys' stories.

As for elephant shooting, we should consider Orwell's essay before returning to 'the Poet'. It recalls an incident from his time in the Burmese police when he was called to deal with a rampaging elephant. 'I had never shot an elephant and never wanted to,' writes Orwell, and explains:

> I had no intention of shooting the elephant – I had merely sent for the rifle to defend myself if necessary. ... As soon as I saw the elephant I knew with perfect certainty that I ought not to shoot him ... at that distance, peacefully eating, the elephant looked no more dangerous than a cow. I thought then and I think now that his attack of 'must' was already passing off; in which case he would merely wander harmlessly about... Moreover, I did not in the least want to shoot him. I decided that I would watch him for a little while to make sure that he did not turn savage again, and then go home (*CWGO* 10: 503).

But because a crowd of around two thousand Burmese has now gathered to watch Orwell and his 'magical' rifle, '... suddenly I realized that I should have to shoot the elephant after all' (ibid. 504).

It is with this that the intellectual cargo of the essay arrives, with its reflections on the futility of colonialism and the peculiarly compromised role it imposes on the 'white man', who has to act as expected of him. For all that, many readers will have found the short-story-like emotional aspect of the piece more memorable. Orwell adds:

But I did not want to shoot the elephant. I watched him beating his bunch of grass against his knees, with that preoccupied grandmotherly air that elephants have. It seemed to me that it would be murder to shoot him (ibid).

But he does shoot him, so as not to lose face in front of the crowd. Instantly, 'a mysterious, terrible change had come over the elephant. … He looked suddenly stricken, shrunken, immensely old, as though the frightful impact of the bullet had paralysed him without knocking him down. … An enormous senility seemed to have settled upon him. … One could have imagined him thousands of years old' (ibid: 505). The elephant refuses to die and Orwell fires more shots, joylessly and wretchedly, until perhaps the most memorable line in the piece: 'He was dying, very slowly and in great agony, but in some world remote from me where not even a bullet could damage him further' (ibid.). Still the elephant does not die, and Orwell leaves the scene saddened and disgusted.

'The Poet', on the other hand, is avid to shoot an elephant. Poets, writes Robinson, like pregnant women, 'have peculiar fancies, and this one wanted to shoot an elephant. I could never understand why…' (Robinson 1942: 113). Robinson and a friend accompany him: 'Neither the friend nor I had any such blood lust, but we felt that the sight might be interesting' (ibid).

People change. But even if, for the sake of argument, we felt that the mature essayist's statement of ten or fifteen years later, 'I had never shot an elephant *and never wanted to*' (*CWGO* 10: 503, my emphasis) might be disingenuous, it still seems unlikely, given the tone and sensibility of Orwell's essay alone, that Robinson's 'Poet', with his callow and almost vandalistic urge to kill an elephant just for the sake of it, is Orwell.

The improbability of the comparison increases, by the end of the elephant-hunting day, with a terrible accident. 'The Poet' never bags an elephant, or if he does we never hear of it. Instead, his rifle – a heavy-calibre elephant gun – goes off and hits a native tracker in the thigh, 'making a ghastly mess of his leg' (Robinson 1942: 114). 'The Poet', who was, 'as might have been expected … not very good in a crisis' (ibid), leaves the wounded man with the rest of the party and sets off for home. Robinson is left to fix up a tourniquet with his revolver lanyard. Again, one might feel this sounds out of character for Orwell. And if Orwell had accidentally wrecked a man's leg with an elephant gun, it is hard to believe that this incident would not be better known; in fact, one also imagines he might even have written about it himself.

This accident, the desire to shoot an elephant, and the stay at Rangoon, in addition to his frail appearance and a pseudonym suggesting that he writes poetry or is 'poetic', comprise virtually all we know of Robinson's 'Poet'. Before finally reiterating that Orwell knew Robinson, Abbott makes a penultimate and more literary point. He notes (Abbott 2006: 46-47) that in his 1934 novel *Burmese Days*, Orwell describes the shattered brain of Flory's dog, after he has shot her before committing suicide himself, as 'like red velvet', and that Robinson's personal opium-smoking area had 'deep red velvet curtains' (which, he concedes, 'may be sheer coincidence').

Abbott further notes similar considerations in both men's thoughts on suicide and disfigurement (ibid: 47). After shooting the dog, Flory looks at the mess his shot has made of the dog's head, and wonders: 'Was that what he would look like?' He decides to shoot himself in the chest instead. Robinson, back in 1925, had thought of blowing his brains out with a gun in his mouth, but realised it would result in 'an unsightly corpse' with the back of the head blown out. Recalling this in *A Modern De Quincey* years later (Robinson 1942: 143), it strikes him: 'It is strange, is it not, that men should be swayed thus in their final hour?' (the consequence, in Robinson's case, was that he botched a shot to the side of his head, blew both eyes out, and lived). Reviewing the book in 1942, Orwell singles out this moment (*CWGO* 14: 34):

> It is profoundly interesting to know what the mind can still contain in the face of apparently certain death – interesting to know, for instance, that a man can be ready to blow his brains out but anxious to avoid a disfiguring wound.

This is a recognisably Orwell idea: it would strike a chord with the man who wrote about Flory and his dog in *Burmese Days*, and the man who was so memorably struck, in his Burmese essay 'A Hanging', by the fact that a man being escorted on his final walk to the gallows would still step over a puddle so as not to get his feet wet (*CWGO* 10: 208).

The memory of the Robinson case, which Orwell must surely have known about, may even haunt Orwell's episode of Flory shooting himself – rather than, say, taking poison or hanging himself – as something at the back of his mind when he wrote *Burmese Days*. But Abbott's point is rather that both men thinking about the state of a corpse after a suicide 'suggests that it was a topic that Robbie [Robinson] had discussed with Blair [Orwell]' (Abbott 2006: 47). This is possible, but it would only confirm that they knew each other, which we already know as our starting point, ever since Orwell's 1942 review of Robinson's book, and not that these thoughts have any connection with the figure of 'the Poet', or link him to Orwell.

Orwell's review of Robinson's book is the origin and virtually sole evidence for a biographical link between them. 'Those who knew the author in Mandalay in 1923,' he writes (*CWGO* 14: 34), were mystified by his turning to opium, and 'Those who knew Captain Robinson in the old days' will be glad to know of 'his continued existence ... cured of the opium habit and apparently well-adjusted and happy...' (ibid 34-35). It is a warm and cordial but not notably enthused review ('amateurishly written'; 'a small but not valueless contribution to the literature of opium') and it keeps a certain distance: the stance on opium, in particular, is a little condescending: this 'debilitating and – in a European – unusual vice'; Robinson 'wanted to escape from real life' (ibid: 34).

Inescapably, Orwell's review means that he must have read Robinson's account of 'the Poet'. Did he recognise himself? If so, what did he make of the elephant incident? Alternatively, did the idea of a link not occur to him – or did he even recognise 'the Poet' as another man he knew? We shall probably never know, but his review seems entirely unruffled; one way or another; he seems to have read about 'the Poet' without so much as raising an eyebrow.

Robinson merits a couple of sentences in several Orwell biographies, but the idea that Orwell is Robinson's 'Poet' muddies the water and needs to be treated with great caution. In particular, Orwell as the protagonist of Robinson's unhappy elephant-hunting incident – avid to blast an elephant for the fun of it, destroying a man's leg with an elephant gun and funking the aftermath – seems unconvincing. If this was true then it would be the most bizarre and extraordinary revelation in Orwell studies for many years. But it is a very weighty 'if'.

Between the possibilities that 'the Poet' is simply someone else, or that he is sheer invention, it is possible that he is a compound from more than one prototype, or even that he began in Robinson's mind as Orwell, taking his poetic vocation and alias from there, before taking off as an essentially fictional character (and as for the idea of elephant shooting, Orwell's celebrated essay had been published a few years before Robinson's autobiography). Orwell may have put Robinson up before Robinson's departure for England. But like the precursor of its title, De Quincey's 1822 *Confessions of an English Opium Eater* (with the strange, dreamlike incident of the Malay, turning up by chance at De Quincey's cottage, and the now disputed existence of the prostitute, Ann) Robinson's book should in any case be treated as a literary artefact; shaped, weighted and very possibly embroidered. Like many autobiographies, to a greater or lesser extent, *A Modern De Quincey* may even be considered to have aspects of 'autobiografiction': a useful term dating back to a 1906 essay by Stephen Reynolds and now associated with the work of Max Saunders (see Saunders 2010: 18, 165-207, and *passim*). The term is really intended to illuminate autobiographical fiction, such as Joyce's *Portrait of the Artist*, but inevitably casts a glow back over the fictional – expressive, imaginative, 'unreliable' – elements in autobiography.

The arguably misleading idea that Orwell is straightforwardly Robinson's 'Poet' has been accompanied by the idea that Robinson is chiefly of interest because he knew Orwell. This is also somewhat pernicious, obscuring Robinson's historical and literary interest in his own right. Robinson returned to Britain, spent four decades as a blind masseur and physiotherapist, and wrote the autobiography that was originally titled – in his 1941 publisher's contract, now in possession of his nephew Jeremy Robinson – *Burma Road* (from the road in Stoke Newington, London, where he discovered he had been born), with its larger sense of a destiny and a spiritual odyssey. The later title, more narrowly sensational in its emphasis on opium, may have been the publisher's suggestion. Robinson finally succeeded in killing himself in 1965, and meanwhile seems to have written nothing more aside from poetry, but his autobiography of his early life, and of his 'going native' as an opium smoker and Buddhist monk, is a minor classic of drug writing, the imperial experience and the British encounter with Buddhism.

REFERENCES

Abbott, Gerry (2004) Introduction, Robinson, H. R., *A Modern De Quincey: Autobiography of an Opium Addict*, Bangkok: Orchid Press, second edition pp ix-xv

Abbott, Gerry (2006) Robbie and the poet, *SOAS Bulletin of Burma Research*, Vol. 4, No. 1, Spring

Meyers, Jeffrey (1972) Orwell in Burma, *American Notes and Queries*, Vol. 11, No. 4. Partially available online at https://sites.google.com/site/orwellsshootinganelephant/home/the-colonial-police-force, accessed on 11 January 2019

Meyers, Jeffrey (2010) *Orwell: Life and Art*, Urbana, Illinois: University of Illinois Press

Moore, Darcy (2018), Orwell and the appeal of opium, *George Orwell Studies*, Vol.3, No.1 pp 83-102

Orwell, George (1997 [1931]) A hanging, *The Complete Works of George Orwell, Vol. 10*, London: Secker and Warburg pp 207-210

Orwell, George (1997 [1936]) Shooting an elephant, *The Complete Works of George Orwell, Vol. 10,* London: Secker and Warburg pp 501-506

Orwell, George (1997 [1942]) Portrait of an addict, *The Complete Works of George Orwell, Vol. 14,* London: Secker and Warburg pp 33-34

Robinson, Captain H. R. (1942) *A Modern De Quincey: An Autobiography*, London, George G. Harrap

Saunders, Max (2010) *Self Impression: Life-Writing, Autobiografiction, and the Forms of Modern Literature*, Oxford: Oxford University Press

Shelden, Michael (1991) *Orwell: The Authorised Biography*, London: Heinemann

Taylor, D. J. (2003) *Orwell: The Life*, London: Chatto & Windus

Taylor, D. J. (2004) Review of H. R. Robinson, *A Modern De Quincey*, second edition, *Times Literary Supplement*, 6 August

Venables, Dione (ed.) (2015) *George Orwell: The Complete Poetry*, UK: Finlay Publishers

ARTICLE

PHIL BAKER

NOTE ON THE CONTRIBUTOR

Phil Baker is a writer based in London. His books include *The Devil is a Gentleman: The Life and Times of Dennis Wheatley*, and *Austin Osman Spare: The Life and Legend of London's Lost Artist*. He has also written an academic book on Samuel Beckett, a cultural history of absinthe, a short critical biography of William S. Burroughs and, more recently, co-edited *Lord of Strange Deaths: The Fiendish World of Sax Rohmer*. He is researching the life of Captain H. R. Robinson for the *Dictionary of National Biography*.

Orwell in Paris: Who Was Ruth Graves?

DARCY MOORE

Among the letters in George Orwell's possession at his death in 1950 was one from an American woman he had known twenty years earlier in Paris. Ruth Graves had, she said, been prompted to write on hearing Animal Farm *(1945) described on the radio as the 'outstanding political satire of all time' (CWGO 20: 150). Who was Ruth Graves and what can we potentially learn about Eric Blair's largely undocumented time in Paris during the dying gasp of* les Années Folles? *Darcy Moore has gone delving – and come up with some fascinating revelations.*

My research into George Orwell's time in Paris, when he was still Eric Blair – the young, unknown, unemployed ex-police officer – faces the same challenge that his many biographers have confronted. There are almost no primary sources and few seemed to know anything about or correspond with the struggling writer at that time.

Only two of Orwell's biographers have mentioned Graves. David Taylor explicitly asked the question, who was Ruth Graves? He noted that she is not hinted at anywhere in Orwell's writings (2004 [2003]: 97). None of his friends knew or mentioned Graves either. We have no record of Orwell ever replying to the caring letter she wrote to him on 23 July 1949 (Graves 1949).

Another biographer, Gordon Bowker (2003: 107-108), thought she was probably a young, affluent American visitor, as Orwell himself had said, 'tourists were as much as part of the scenery of Paris as tobacco kiosks and tin urinals' and tended to spend money like water.

We do not know for certain when Graves became aware that Eric Blair, the young man she had been friends with in Paris during the late 1920s, was George Orwell, the writer, but it was probably not until 1949, when she listened to the radio broadcast.

Graves's letter indicated she was looking forward to reading *Nineteen Eighty-Four* and that they had a mutual friend, Edith Morgan. She also knew 'Mrs Adam', Orwell's bohemian Aunt Nellie, who lived in Paris and was married to the Esperantist, Eugène

Adam (Lanti) (see Forster 1982). Most significantly for biographers, Graves fondly remembered 'the very good talk of a tall young man in a wide-brimmed pair of Breton hats, who was as kind as he was keen of mind' recalling:

> … those Saturday evenings in Paris, when we took turns about the dinner, and the hours of good talk later in my little cluttered place in rue de la Grande Chaumière. You showed me sketches of your experiences – some of the material I recognised when 'Down and Out in Paris and London' came out. Perhaps I was your first critic? (Graves 1949).

Graves's 'little cluttered place' is near Boulevard Montparnasse, thus approximately a twenty-minute walk from where Orwell's residence at 6 Rue Pot de Fer, in the fifth arrondissement, was located.

It was also evident from her letter, written six months before Orwell died, that Graves knew her friend was seriously ill. She offered to procure medicine but knowing that there might be difficulties importing it to England, volunteered to act as courier. They must have been very good friends or, less generously, the allure of Orwell's fame burned brightly. Tellingly, Graves also confides in her letter that, since returning to America ten years ago on the outbreak of WWII, she still did not feel at home (ibid).

BLAIR IN PARIS

Orwell, the quintessentially English writer, was always interested in his French ancestry. He was very literate in the language and R. N. Raimbault, the translator for *Down and Out in Paris and London* (1933), told Orwell his written French, in their letters, was 'not merely correct, but elegant' (Orwell 2006: 13). In his memoirs, Anthony Powell (1983) expressed a belief that 'Orwell's quarter-French ancestry' was important to both his 'temperament and approach to writing'.

Eric Blair moved to France ostensibly to live cheaply while he kick-started his career as a writer. But after five years serving the British empire as a police officer in Burma (1922-1927) Orwell must have fantasised about escaping to the cultural mecca of Paris, as many thousands of expatriates endeavouring to paint, write or – at the very least – affect a bohemian lifestyle had done before him. He wrote, in his first novel, *Burmese Days* (1997 [1934]: 132-133):

> Paris – it's all a kind of jumble of pictures in my mind; cafés and boulevards and artists' studios and Villon and Baudelaire and Maupassant all mixed up together. … Sitting in cafés with foreign art students, drinking white wine and talking about Marcel Proust?

Orwell claimed to have written two unsuccessful novels (and regretted destroying the manuscripts) during his time in Paris. Some of his first published articles, written in French, appeared in *Monde* and *Le Progrès Civique*. We also know that he wrote at least three short stories that were never published and the feedback received suggested his work was 'immature … you deal with sex too much in your writings' (*CWGO* 10: 113). Orwell also reviewed a biography of Baudelaire, the dissolute poet of modernity, for the *Adelphi* after departing France (Blair 1933).

Even though evidence suggests Orwell worked hard on his writing, I always wondered whom he spent his spare time with during the dying gasp of *les Années Folles*, 'the Crazy Years'? There is a lack of primary sources for the eighteen months, in 1928-1929, that Eric Blair spent in the capital. In fact, letters (mostly rejection letters) from editors, are close to all that really exists (*CWGO* 10: 113-114).

There are a few clues from interviews that Stephen Wadhams conducted in 1983, including with Louis Bannier, an Esperantist and close associate of Eugène Adam, Aunt Nellie's husband (Wadhams 1983). There are some interesting insights from Mabel Fierz (who knew him in Southwold and London rather than Paris) into Orwell's 'girlfriends'. This included one 'trollop' that she claimed Orwell would have married, except she absconded with his possessions (ibid).

Orwell's first published book, *Down and Out in Paris and London* (1933), is reportage but largely focuses on his last months in the city. Orwell always said the book was based on lived experiences and interestingly, he illustrated this by annotating a friend's copy (Shelden 1991: 146). It is worth remembering that biographer and Orwell scholar, Bernard Crick (1992 [1980]), cautioned against conflating literary works with the man. Other sources are essential.

LOOKING FOR RUTH

One would have thought that having Graves's name and knowing she was an American in inter-war Paris would be enough to trace Orwell's friend, who so admired his 'Breton hats' (Graves 1949). Not so, it would seem. However, since the last major biographies were published in 2003, on the centenary of Orwell's birth, online databases have improved significantly.

Knowing that Graves returned to the United States in October 1939, from Peter Davison's editorial notes in the final volume of *The Complete Works of George Orwell* (1998), I started searching the passenger records of vessels bound for the USA. This simple line of enquiry proved very fruitful.

A Ruth Eleanor Graves, born 8 January 1884, was listed as passenger on the S.S. Saint John. This steamer departed for New

York, from Bordeaux, on 14 October 1939. She appeared to be travelling alone and was recorded as 'single' rather than 'married'. There are no other Ruth Graves returning to New York from France during this period but was this fifty-five-year-old passenger, who would have been in her mid-forties when she knew Eric Blair, *the* Ruth Graves?

Besides her birth date, I now knew *this* Ruth was born in Lexington, Illinois, and that her hometown was Wichita, Kansas. Her passport was easily found (*Ancestry.com:* 21 February 1924-25 February 1924) and indicated she likely departed for Paris from New York in early 1924. Did that mean she resided in Paris for fifteen years? If so, Ruth Graves was neither 'young' nor 'a tourist', as suggested by Bowker (op cit: 108).

WHO WAS SHE REALLY?

Photographs, even those for passports, can prove hypnotic. I stared at Ruth Graves, who did not look directly back at me from New York in 1924 but gazed slightly off to her left. She looked surprisingly modern. Examining the passport more closely, I noticed that the section of the form for the 'object of visit' indicated that Graves did not see herself as a tourist. Written in a neat, cursive hand, was 'study of art'.

Nearly convinced that this was very likely *the* Ruth Graves, returned from a very lengthy French sojourn to avoid war, I searched online but without much luck. Did she become an artist or was she merely another wealthy dilettante? The Archives of American Art, a bureau of the Smithsonian Institution, and Google seemed to confirm the latter. Then, a hardworking librarian's years of research saved the day.

Susan Craig, Art and Architecture Librarian at the University of Kansas, had compiled a *Biographical Dictionary of Kansas Artists (active before 1945)* published in 2009. This was the lead I needed to leap over the research brick wall to truly find Ruth. *The Genealogy of the Greenlee Families in America* (1908) cleared the fog of Graves's ancestry and a local newspaper, the *Wichita Eagle,* provided most of the treasure. An article in *The Shocker*, a publication for alumni of Wichita State University, was also invaluable (Perleberg and Platt 2008).

RUTH ELEANOR GRAVES (1884-1964)

The only child of Walter and Mary Graves, Ruth grew up in Wichita and was educated at Fairmount College (now Wichita State University). Her father was a physician and one of the college's board of trustees. Mary (née Brooks, then Mrs Paddock) was born into a French-speaking community in Sherbrooke, Canada, and had a son to a previous marriage before being widowed and marrying

Walter. Graves's mother was a keen reader, founding the Fairmount Library Club after the previous community collection of books had been stolen.

From an early age Graves exhibited an interest in art and a determination to succeed. Her father related an anecdote to a local newspaper that illustrates his daughter's initiative. Walter explained that 'modelling clay' for his young daughter was just not available (in late nineteenth century Wichita) so this small child simply solved the problem by successfully making her own from a recipe.

Often called 'Eleanor', rather than 'Ruth', by her father and in the newspapers, Graves was regularly celebrated for her determination, artistic and writing talent. As a school girl she was remarkably self-reliant. There is a report in a local newspaper about Graves as a young student, in terrible weather, walking six miles to attend classes because of her passion for learning (*Wichita Daily Eagle* 1899).

I was struck by the attitude of Walter, Ruth's father, towards his daughter. He had come to believe that it was very undesirable to repress the artistic instincts of any individual and encouraged his only child to pursue her passion for art. Indeed, Ruth Graves had a privileged life and was extremely well-educated. One portrait, when she was about eighteen, shows an expensively dressed, sophisticated and confident young woman. She was the art editor of college publications, such as *The Sunflower* and *Parnassus*, which contained her line drawings, including a stunning, gold-leaf representation of Mount Parnassus on the cover. Interestingly, Orwell at the same age was contributing to *The Election Times* and *College Days* while at Eton.

Graves, with her aptitude for art, graduated from the college in 1903 and moved to Chicago. She spent a number of years studying at both the University of Chicago and the School of the Art Institute before working independently teaching. She continued her studies by moving to New York City and commenced a long association with the Art Students League of New York (records indicate she won a scholarship and later supported the institution financially until her death). During these formative years, in the first two decades of the twentieth century, her instructors commented that Graves was an extraordinarily diligent young woman, highly independent and original:

> Before she had had anything except the mere rudiments of drawing, she showed intense earnestness in everything pertaining to art. She was eager to learn and one of the most interested pupils I ever had (Elizabeth Sprague) (*Wichita Eagle* 1926).

ARTICLE

If she could imitate, she would get along faster at first. But she is a strong individualist. Professor Seymour (ibid).

In 1904, it was noted in the local newspaper that 'Miss Graves' had been chosen as a replacement teacher in Wichita and then was teaching in Chicago, from 1904, where she was studying art (*Wichita Daily Eagle*). Once again, like Orwell, they both needed to teach while pursuing artistic goals. In 1914, Graves's artwork was displayed in the window of 'Martin's Art Store' (*Wichita Beacon* 1914). Her technical innovation is highlighted in the local newspaper as the 'pictures are unique' and she is 'painting in oil on paper' to create monotypes. The 'delicate beauty of a well-executed water colour and a freshness of tint seldom attained' is reportedly a huge improvement compared to using canvas (ibid).

A letter Graves wrote to her father, twelve years before she knew Orwell, shows a talented writer. On Christmas Day 1916, this remarkable letter from 'Eleanor' Graves was published in *The Wichita Beacon*. Graves wrote from Lancaster, New Hampshire, where she was spending the winter:

> I have seen the Flume at last. It was a little late for the trip and I supposed I would see only the skeleton of things to clothe with imagination, but November has its charm as well as June. All thru the Flume, the wet rocks were plastered with leaves, here and there was a flock of October glory.
>
> The paths were beautiful. The forest was a mist of bare trees, warmed by the russet boughs of the graceful winter beech and the thick leaf carpet of softer brown – the purple of the mountain peeping thru from beyond.
>
> The pool was like a huge green gem. Mist was floating and scurrying about the tops of the mountains, and the Echo and Profile Lakes were silver under it.
>
> It seemed just the time to see the Old Man of the Mountains. He belongs to greys with his stern face, like some sharp-featured old pioneer. What legends must have been woven about him? Generations wander thru the valleys and carry on little enterprises and always he is there in the sunshine or the mist gazing out over their heads into distance.
>
> The snow up here hasn't anything on white frost. It comes like September dew and glistens on every twig and pine needle. I woke the other morning to see this exquisite fretwork against the most wonderful pink dawn from behind the mountains. The Little Folk of the Ice King never did such work as this.

The letter goes on to describe experiences in Quebec.

I stood there on the steps and looked back over the landmarks of bygone days. I saw the missionaries, Indians, voyageurs and dashing adventurers of the old St. Lawrence days. The sky was a dark blue and the river a darker sliver. Lights like those in Never-Never Land twinkled faint and fainter along the bank until they were lost in darkness. Above me the orchestra was playing and the promenade was becoming gay with people.

Mountain Hill Street was another favourite of mine in Quebec. I stood by the post office steps under the sign of the Golden Dog and looked down, watching the picturesque old carts clatter up and down the cobble stones. It is a graceful street as it curves around the rampart of the lower town. Gray-green willows peep over the majestic gray walls at the left. On the right the shops descend like steps. Between them you catch a tiny glimpse of the river.

This, too, is best at twilight, when the golden haze comes from the shops and carts with their shadows take on romantic shapes.

Sous-le-Cap Street is best in the bright sunshine, tho there are the same smells at any time of the day, and the same shrill cries of the children signalling the approach of the penny-bearing tourist. Green petticoats, red table cloths and patchwork quilts hung across the streets add cheer to the weather-beaten stairs and passageways between the buildings, only a wagon-width apart.

There were little picture houses, such as the cardinal, in gorgeous silks, pale-faced and Franciscans friars in their heavy robes, beautiful French chidden with their sense of dress down even to the poorest, a great pile of carrots in the open Champlain market, many scenes that I remember from my excursions.

Following one of the hard Canadian thunderstorms, I went out for a walk and got lost. In a French town, no lady is out after nightfall. I was down among the shipyards and I began to feel a little uncertain. I soon found a little French boy that I knew and he guided me back to my station.

In the rain I had ruined my last decent pair of shoes. Shoes are doomed in Quebec. The rain completes what hills and cobblestones begin. Across the narrow sidewalks run many little rivers which no-one has thought to train under the walk, just as ice is left at everyone's door because no-one has thought to deliver it in any other way.

During the ten days I spent in Quebec, I had been away not only from noise and ugliness but also from efficiency. I was glad to get across the river again for in the morning I could see the gray city on the cliffs once more. I had an excellent chance to say

ARTICLE

goodbye to it. My ride to Sherbrooke was charming as the ride to Quebec, but nothing satisfies after the visions I have had in Quebec.

One can see why a proud father had the letter published. Graves has a poetic turn of phrase as well as an observant eye for people and places. It makes one rather hungry to find the weekly postcards she wrote to her father from Paris or other letters to friends.

Feeling disappointed with her lack of success in New York, Graves moved to Paris in 1924, where she was to live for the next fifteen years. She had some reasonably immediate professional success exhibiting three paintings at the prestigious Société Nationale des Beaux-Arts (National Society for Fine Arts), known as 'the Salon' or 'Salon de Paris', in 1926. We know, from a celebratory article in *The Wichita Eagle* newspaper back home (*Sunday Magazine*, 13 June 1926), Graves paid $30 a month to rent a studio in Paris and was quoted as saying it 'would be considered quite pretentious in New York'. This pretentiousness had paid dividends.

It is probably not completely safe to surmise this studio was located at the address, Rue de la Grande Chaumière, mentioned in her letter to Orwell. One would usually assume that such a studio was in a separate location but was Graves able to afford a small apartment too? It is worth noting that the Italian artist Amedeo Modigliani (1884-1920), opium-addicted and indulging in a wild lifestyle, had had a studio in the same street before his death, a few years before Graves's arrival in Montparnasse (see Salmon 1961). Graves registered with officials and the French Police Archives list her as entering France on 11 November 1924 and residing at '12 rue de Bréa in 6e arrondissement de Paris'.

Another American, the translator Samuel Putnam, in his memoir, *Paris Was Our Mistress* (1947), vividly described the neighbourhood:

> … the Montparnasse we knew: a weird little land crowded with artists, alcoholics, prostitutes, pimps, poseurs, college boys, tourists, society slummers, spendthrifts, beggars, homosexuals, drug addicts, nymphomaniacs, sadists, masochists, thieves, gamblers, confidence men, mystics, takers, paranoiacs, political refugees, anarchists, 'Dukes' and 'Countesses', men and women without a country; a land filled with a gaiety sometimes real and often feigned, filled with sorrow, suffering, poverty, frustration, bitterness, tragedy, suicide. Not only was there never any place like it; Montparnasse itself had never been before and never will be again what it was in the 1920's. For it was essentially a part of the first après-guerre, and from 1929 on it began dying.

One of the paintings she exhibited in 1926 was a cityscape of Paris, viewed from Notre Dame, which Graves later presented to her alma mater on the fiftieth anniversary of her graduation (where it is still prominently displayed). One of the other three paintings from this exhibition was a portrait of Joel Martin Nichols Jr. (1895-1991), an American veteran of WWI, journalist and published author when Graves knew him. The story of how they met, reported in the local newspaper, is of its time:

> Early one morning, Mr. Nichols, searching for the abode of a friend, wandered into the labyrinths of the Latin quarter, where the artists congregate. Miss Graves had locked herself out of her studio, and while she was trying to boost a too-stout janitor through the window so he could unlock her door, Mr. Nichols spied her. Mr. Nichols gallantly relieved the situation by opening the door himself, and remained to pose for Miss Graves on the promise of a cup of 'real American coffee' (*Wichita Eagle* 1926).

Interestingly, Nichols published many short stories in pulp magazines, including *Weird Tales*. His writing was popular with fans. He went on to work in advertising on returning to New York in 1926 and was to become the director of the Federal Advertising Agency. I can find no record of him in Paris during Orwell's time but it is likely they would have had much in common. The long-lived Nichols also wrote to his dying day.

In 1928, it appears that Graves exhibited for a second time at the Société Nationale des Beaux-Arts in Paris. Orwell arrived in Paris during early April 1928 so it is possible he saw her work then. I was surprised to discover that besides Graves, fifty-four other Americans were featured during this time including twelve painters or sculptors from the 'middle-west' and two other artists from 'Illinois' (Ernest Hemingway was from this state too and it is theoretically possible they met).

I was even more surprised to learn that the 1926 census suggests Paris was home to nearly 10,000 American expatriates and probably many more who were not officially recorded. Not all of them would be visiting Algiers, as Graves did in 1926, to stay with a daughter of J. P. Morgan in a mansion where she was able to appreciate the 'North African colour' (*Wichita Eagle* 1926).

Graves, on returning to America in late 1939, never married and lived most of her life in New York. Her father passed away in 1941 and Graves's mother died years before when her daughter was studying in Chicago (where many of the extended family of her mother's previous marriage lived). There is a good record of Graves's addresses documented via her association with the Art Students League of New York. In 1940, she had become a life member.

DARCY MOORE

There are only three surviving paintings by Graves that I have been able to locate. There must be more but the Morrison Library in Wichita, which housed thirty-two of her artworks, burnt to the ground in July 1964, two months after the artist's death. Graves donated these paintings in the 1930s so possibly some were moved before the fire. Two landscape oil paintings sold in 2012 for $250 each. Only one of them was signed. One suspects that Graves's work may increase in value, if anyone can find her paintings.

THE LETTER

The final confirmation of the identity of this American woman, who wrote to George Orwell in July 1949, as Ruth Eleanor Graves (1884-1964) from Wichita, Kansas, was made by comparing the original letter, supplied courtesy of the Orwell Archive in London, with her 1924 passport application. The signatures matched. One is carefully inked for a passport and the other scrawled, a more casual signature for a letter. Twenty-five years separate the two signatures but they are remarkably similar.

Graves's six-page letter has information not mentioned by Orwell scholars Peter Davison, David Taylor or Gordon Bowker. This is simply because when the letter, probably not looked at in the last 16 years or so, is examined with the knowledge of the actual correspondent's identity, useful new information can be gleaned from the text.

Graves' address was '51 West 69th St New York 23' which is a four-story Brownstone, with twenty units, located in Lincoln Square. The Art Students League of New York was a pleasant stroll through Central Park away. It would be fascinating to compare the current Google Street View, where one sees too many cars and some amusing graffiti, with a historic photograph from the mid-twentieth century. It is a very desirable residential location in NYC.

Graves opened her letter saying she started writing it two years ago when Orwell had popped into her mind. She jokes about hoping the 'psychic phenomenon boys' can figure out why he appeared there for no reason. Many keen readers of Orwell's work may not know that this most rational of writers was quite superstitious and interested in such phenomena. It is probable that Graves included this whimsical or throwaway line as they had likely discussed paranormal phenomena twenty years previously.

A minor point but I will correct it for the record. It seems that Davison was wrong in suggesting Graves had read all Orwell's essays (*CWGO* 20: 150). My reading of her letter is that she had read all Orwell's work but *not* his essays. Graves's handwriting is very legible and I am confident this is correct (Graves 1949).

Prising between the lines for information about the nature of their friendship, the following passage in Graves's letter is particularly fascinating:

> I came back to America in 1939, in October, but do not feel that I am at home yet. New York has been most inhospitable – and I am a rebel in a world that has become so regimented that I can find no foothold in it. I have all the more a desire to read your latest book – I know I shall echo it with all my heart. I have been harmed personally by this trend that lurks in more than just high places.

Does Graves allude to the politics of the art world in New York City when she bemoans such regimentation and her lack of a 'foothold'? What else could it be a reference to if not her art? Maybe this is a more personal issue relating to sexuality? Graves never married, perhaps she was a lesbian? To what extent would this be an impediment to success in her chosen profession in 1940s USA? Were her father's comments about the 'undesirability of repressing' the artistic urge in his daughter to be read as acknowledgment of Graves's sexuality?

There are many other questions worth considering regarding Graves not feeling 'at home' after a decade. Why did she spend so long in France? Her passport notes she was visiting to study art and we know that she returned on the outbreak of war but what kept her in Paris? Her police registration card lists her as a student too. The 1920s in Paris was a period of great artistic ferment and many creative Americans enjoyed personal freedom to drink alcohol, experiment with drugs and sexuality. As Shari Benstock highlights in *Women of the Left Bank* (1986), there was an artistic and intellectual licence granted that was just not possible in America or Britain.

Graves mentioned in the letter that she knew Orwell's Aunt Nellie (Mrs Adam) had returned to London from France. This suggests she had corresponded with others in their circle of friends and acquaintances. It occurred to me to map where Aunt Nellie and her husband lived in their top-floor flat at 14 Avenue Corbéra, in the twelfth arrondissement. Orwell would have had to cross the Seine, passing Graves's studio en route to the Adam residence.

Reading the complete six-page letter provides a sense of Ruth, the person and why Orwell, as a young man, would have been intellectually attracted to the artist twenty years his senior. Graves's biographical details also illuminate why Orwell would have found the older woman an attractively intelligent companion. Graves's personal and professional life is deserving of study – not just because of this connection to Orwell – but in her own right.

DARCY MOORE THE SIGNIFICANCE OF ERIC BLAIR'S RELATIONSHIP WITH RUTH GRAVES?

Orwell, in his seminal 1940 essay on American expatriate Henry Miller, *Inside the Whale*, wrote amusingly about Paris when the exchange-value of the franc was low:

> Paris was invaded by such a swarm of artists, writers, students, dilettanti, sight-seers, debauchees and plain idlers as the world has probably never seen. In some quarters of the town the so-called artists must actually have outnumbered the working population – indeed, it has been reckoned that in the late 'twenties there were as many as 30,000 painters in Paris, most of them impostors. The populace had grown so hardened to artists that gruff-voiced Lesbians in corduroy breeches and young men in Grecian or medieval costume could walk the streets without attracting a glance, and along the Seine banks by Notre Dame it was almost impossible to pick one's way between the sketching-stools (*CWGO* 12: 86).

Ruth Graves, having lived and exhibited in Paris for several years before Orwell arrives, was not an 'impostor'. The young Blair would have learnt a great deal from the older woman, devoted to art, who was to spend so many years as an expatriate. We do not know if she wore 'corduroy breeches' or perhaps joked with Orwell about the trend. This highly-educated American woman (and her friend, Edith Morgan) were certainly not 'down and out' nor prostitutes and it seems likely that Orwell was associating with a well-heeled, artistic milieu in Paris far more often than he would have us believe or his later reputation suggested. For example, in 1931, Orwell wrote to T. S. Eliot at Faber & Faber about his suitability for translating particular French novels:

> I have just read a rather interesting French novel called *Á la Belle de Nuit*, by Jacques Roberti. It is the story of a prostitute, quite true to life so far as one can judge, & most ruthlessly told, but not a mere exploitation of a dirty subject. It seems to me worth translating, & if Messrs. Faber & Faber would like to try a translation I think I could do the job as well as most people. I don't pretend to have a scholarly knowledge of French, but I am used to mixing in the kind of French society described in the novel, & I know French slang, if not well, better than the majority of Englishmen. I don't know whether such a book would sell, but I believe Zola's novels sell in England, & this author seems to have some resemblances to Zola (*CWGO* 10: 235).

Eliot did not take Orwell up on his offer to translate *Á la Belle de Nuit*. That was completed in the USA by Samuel Putnam, who described Montparnasse so vividly in his memoir. His translation of the novel was titled, *Without Sin* (1933) which contrasts significantly to the choice made by Mary Ford, another translator, *Houses of the Lost* (1932).

Orwell's first book, *Down and Out in London and Paris,* was reviewed positively and sold well, being reprinted twice during the month it was released. It was the beginning of Orwell's reputation for being a writer who more explored proletarian experiences than those of his own class.

Considering our limited information about who Orwell knew in Paris, his connections via Nellie's husband Eugène Adam are important to making a map of acquaintances. These included the first person to publish his writing, Henri Barbusse, who was author of the anti-war novel, *Le Feu* (1916), and editor of the left-wing periodical *Monde*. He wrote the first biography of Stalin in 1935. It is worth noting that Barbusse was accused of espionage in October 1928 (*The Times* 1928) so it is probably not too surprising that MI5 started a file on Orwell in January 1929 (*Discovery.nationalarchives.gov.uk*). Orwell must have also known René Nicole and Henri Dumay who published several of his earliest articles in the radical journal, *Le Progrès Civique* (Bowker 2003: 107).

One of the interesting additional facts in Graves's letter was that she still communicated with Edith Morgan twenty years after living in Paris. I noted that she was contacted by her friend in 1948: 'I have heard briefly from Edith Morgan, at Christmas. She was visiting in Rome' (Graves 1949). Who was this mutual friend? I am tantalisingly close to confirming the identify of Edith Morgan. Mostly this has been done by eliminating who she is not and there are many possible 'Edith Morgans'. It has been frustrating and difficult as several times it seemed the mystery was solved.

I am currently waiting on a document, stored in a French archive, to be located and copied. I think it possible that Edith was an artist who exhibited in Paris during 1928. If this is confirmed there is more chance that information about Eric Blair will be uncovered. I have pondered over Graves's letter when she says: 'I can hardly expect you to remember me after more than twenty years' but then goes on to write about taking turns with dinner and 'the hours of good talk late in my little cluttered place'. How would Orwell forget such a relationship or perhaps she is just being polite? Either way it is clear that there was no further communication after Orwell left Paris in December 1929 until Graves wrote in July 1949.

Sadly, Ruth Eleanor Graves died in a New York State mental hospital in 1964. She was probably suffering from an undiagnosed dementia, perhaps Alzheimer's disease, unable to 'treasure all the memories' of her years in Paris. I am yet to find her will but an obituary (*Wichita Eagle* 1964) lists a niece, Miss Beatrice Paddock – who later died in 1997 aged 95.

CONCLUSION

My research into Ruth Graves continues apace and gives some cause for hope that more evidence about Orwell's time in Paris will emerge. At the very least, the hunt is *always fun* when there are so many interesting questions to be answered. Did Orwell reply to Graves's letter? Did Edith Morgan, their mutual friend, correspond with Graves? Did Graves keep diaries and letters? If so, where are they to be located? Do the 'weekly' postcards from Paris to her father survive?

One very important question to my mind is did Graves sketch or paint Orwell, maybe in his 'Breton hat'? One does get the sense of a joke, or gentle ribbing, being shared in her letter to Orwell. The visual image (of the rarely photographed) Eric Blair wearing this style of head-ware has occupied more of my time than warranted (and I now have some expertise in the evolution of the Breton cap from the nineteenth century). However, I am still uncertain if the 'wide-brimmed pair of Breton hats' Graves mentions are the style of cap popularised in the sixties by The Beatles (perhaps even earlier by Vladimir Lenin) or if it is some other kind of 'hat' that is less familiar to contemporary readers? Visualising Blair, perhaps with a beard (as there is some suggestion, he was not always clean-shaven) is made very possible if he wore this cap at a jaunty angle … but I digress.

- Originally published at my blog with photographs, newspaper clippings and links to further reading: http://www.darcymoore.net/tag/ruth-eleanor-graves/

REFERENCES

Ancestry.com (n. d.) US passport applications, 1795-1925, Washington DC: National Archives and Records Administration (NARA) 21 February 1924-25 February 1924

Ancestry.com (n. d.) New York, Passenger and Crew Lists (including Castle Garden and Ellis Island), 1820-1957. Year: 1939; Arrival: New York, New York; Microfilm Serial: T715, 1897-1957; Microfilm Roll: Roll 6413; Line: 4; Page Number: 11

Benstock, Shari (1986) *Women of the Left Bank*, Texas: University of Texas Press

Blair, Eric Arthur (1933) Review: Enid Starkie's *Baudelaire*, *CWGO* 10 pp 320-21. Originally published *The Adelphi*, Vol. 6, No. 5, August

Bowker, Gordon (2003) *Inside George Orwell*, New York: Palgrave Macmillan

Craig, Susan (2009) *Biographical Dictionary of Kansas Artists (active before 1945)*, Lawrence, Kansas. Available online at http://kuscholarworks.ku.edu/dspace/bitstream/1808/1028/4/BDKAversion2.pdf, accessed on 12 January 2019

Crick, Bernard (1992 [1980]) *George Orwell: A Life*, Harmondsworth, Middlesex: Penguin, second edition

Orwell, George (2006) *The Lost Orwell, Being a Supplement to the Complete Works of George Orwell*, Davison, Peter (ed.) London: Timewell Press Limited

Discovery.nationalarchives.gov.uk (2018) Special Branch file on Eric Blair alias George Orwell, author and journalist, *The National Archives*, MEPO 38/69. Available online at http://discovery.nationalarchives.gov.uk/details/r/C10881756, accessed on 22 September 2018

Forster, Peter G. (1982) *The Esperanto Movement*, The Netherlands: Mouton Publishers

Graves, Ruth (1949) Letter 23 July, Orwell Archive

Greenlee, Ralph Stebbins and Greenlee, Robert Lemuel (1908) *Genealogy of the Greenlee families in America* (privately printed)

Orwell, George (1945) *Animal Farm*, London: Martin Secker & Warburg Ltd.

Orwell, George (1997 [1933]) *Down and Out in London and Paris, The Complete Works of George Orwell*, Vol.1, London: Secker & Warburg pp 124-126

Orwell, George (1997 [1934]) *Burmese Days, The Complete Works of George Orwell*, Vol. 2, London: Secker & Warburg

Orwell, George (1998) *A Kind of Compulsion (1903-1936), The Complete Works of George Orwell, Vol. 10*, Davison, Peter (ed.) London: Secker & Warburg

Orwell, George (1998) *A Patriot After All (1940-1941), The Complete Works of George Orwell, Vol. 12*, Davison, Peter (ed.) London: Secker & Warburg

Orwell, George (1998) *Our Job is to Make Life Worth Living (1949-1950), The Complete Works of George Orwell, Vol. 20*, Davison, Peter (ed.) London: Secker & Warburg

Perleberg, Anna and Platt, George (2008) A girl who went from Wichita to Paris and won success, *The Shocker*. Available online at http://wsu.wichita.edu/the-shocker/story.php?eid=1&id=231#.XDm8lM8zbOT, accessed on 12 January 2019]

Powell, Anthony (1983) *To Keep the Ball Rolling: The Memoirs of Anthony Powell*, London: Penguin Books Ltd

Putnam, Samuel (1947) *Paris Was Our Mistress: Memoirs of a Lost and Found Generation*, New York: Viking Press

Salmon, André (1961) *Modigliani – A Memoir*, New York: Jonathan Cape Ltd

Shelden, Michael (1991) *Orwell: The Authorised Biography*, London: William Heinemann Ltd

Taylor, D. J. (2004 [2003]) *Orwell – The Life*, London: Vintage

The Times (1928) M. Barbusse accused of espionage, 21 October

Wadhams, Stephen (1983) *Unpublished Recordings from CBC Radio* (courtesy of the Orwell Society)

Wadhams, Stephen (1984) *Remembering Orwell*, Harmondsworth, Middlesex: Penguin

Wichita Beacon (1914) Wichita girl is an Artist, 27 February

Wichita Daily Eagle (1899) Fairmount Notes, 19 February

Wichita Daily Eagle (1904) 5 January

Wichita Daily Eagle (1904) 20 November

Wichita Eagle (1916) Paints fairyland in letter home, 25 December

Wichita Eagle (1926) A girl who went from Wichita to Paris and won success, *Sunday Magazine*, 13 June (courtesy of Wichita Public Library)

Wichita Eagle (1964) Ruth Eleanor Graves: Obituary, 29 May (courtesy of Wichita Public Library)

DARCY MOORE NOTE ON THE CONTRIBUTOR

Darcy Moore is a deputy principal at a secondary school in New South Wales. He teaches English and History and has worked as an academic in post-graduate teacher education at the University of Wollongong. His interest in Orwell began at school, thirty-five years ago, when he was enthralled by *Animal Farm* and *Nineteen Eighty-Four*. He is currently working on two books about Orwell. He blogs at darcymoore.net and his Twitter handle is @Darcy1968. His Orwell collection can be accessed at darcymoore.net/orwell-collection/.

Gordon Bowker: So wonderfully insightful into Orwell the man and his writings

RICHARD LANCE KEEBLE

Richard Lance Keeble pays tribute to Orwell biographer Gordon Bowker who died in January 2019.

Given that George Orwell specifically indicated in his will that no biography of him should be written, how does one justify just such an undertaking? One of Orwell's biographers, Gordon Bowker, who died aged 84 in January 2019, clearly thought a lot about this question. And in the end, his answer is tightly argued and persuasive.

He writes: 'He was certainly not antagonistic to the genre, as some have suggested. In fact, in his reviews and letters there is ample evidence that he valued literary biography as a means of illuminating an author's work.' And in a review of Lewis Mumford's biography of Melville, Orwell perhaps indicates the kind of work he may have liked: Mumford's 'analytical, interpretative method' exploring his ideas, his feelings, his urges, his vision of life was the one he favoured.[1]

Significantly, in the Preface of his biography of George Orwell (London: Little Brown, 2003) Gordon Bowker sets out his ambitions with these perceptive comments:

> Orwell himself was a man with deep feelings, which he attempted as far as possible to conceal. Yet, as he admitted, it was emotion that provided the driving force of his creativity. The main thrust of this book will be to reach down as far as possible to the roots of that emotional life, to get as close as possible to the dark sources mirrored in his work (p. xii).

And through the course of the 495-page text he succeeds in following Mumford's 'analytical, interpretative method', delving deep into Orwell the man – providing original and often profound insights into his writings and complex personality. Bowker's prose is always clear yet densely packed with meticulously researched information – and throughout he displays a deep knowledge of the politics and broader culture of Orwell's times.

RICHARD LANCE KEEBLE

Indeed, for an insightful, concise yet wide-ranging overview of Orwell, there is perhaps little to compare with Bowker's six-page Preface to the biography. He talks of how Orwell was 'fascinated by how things work, from pieces of machinery to human societies. … This intuitive grasp of social patterns and processes, his sociological imagination, enabled him to develop into a writer of vision' (p. xii). Despite his reputation for honesty, 'he had a deceptive streak' (p. xiii):

> He deceived fellow tramps about his identify and true circumstances, he kept his family ignorant of what he was doing; he deliberately kept some of his friends apart in order to present them with different faces; he was deceptive in his sexual relationships; he concealed his true feelings behind a mask of reserve. The revelation that he co-operated with the IRD [the state's secret propaganda unit] left some of his old friends feeling badly deceived as to his true nature. He deliberately concealed himself behind a pseudonym.

He was also a man full of contradictions: 'So while he was against private schools, disliked Scots, and was a staunch atheist, he put his adopted son down for Westminster, chose to live among Scots on Jura and asked to be buried according to the rites of the Church of England' (p. xiv).

Bowker is particularly interesting throughout the biography when examining Orwell's sexuality. Here he writes: 'Like his fictional heroes, he had difficulty approaching women. In his teens, he was rebuffed by a childhood sweetheart; in Burma he indulged with prostitutes and is said to have had a child by a Burmese girl; in Paris in 1928 he lived for a while with a "trollop". … Although part of him wished to emulate sexually unbridled writers like D. H. Lawrence, James Joyce and Henry Miller, the social and political climate of his age and the harsh obscenity laws propelled him towards literary puritanism' (ibid).

Bowker is at pains to acknowledge the unique insights thrown up by the previous biographies: Bernard Crick (1980) stressed the political context; Michael Shelden (1991) highlighted Orwell the literary man; Meyers (2000) 'acknowledged more the inner man' (p. xiii). And throughout, Bowker acknowledges as a crucial source, the recent publication of the 20-volume *Collected Works of George Orwell*, edited by Peter Davison (D. J. Taylor's award-winning biography was also to appear in 2003 so could not be acknowledged). But Bowker also turns up new and important information.

For instance, there is a lot new here on the family background of Orwell's mother. Her father, Frank Limouzin, was a timber merchant in Limoges, France, before emigrating to Burma in the late 1850s with his wife, Eliza. Ida, Orwell's mother, was their sixth (of eight) children who grew up in Moulmein, marrying Richard Walmsley Blair, a lowly sub-deputy opium agent, in June 1897. At the time Ida was 22, Richard 39. Eric Arthur Blair, their second child, was born on 25 June 1903. So much is already well known. Now Bowker goes on to reveal how the Limouzins of Moulmein sadly fell on hard times: Franks' boat-building company collapsed and so he moved into the rice business, 'losing much of his money in the process' (p. 10).

> His long-deceased brother William had co-habited with an Indian woman; now, in 1899, his second eldest son, Ida's brother Frank, fathered a child by a Burmese girl, Mah Hlim. There could well have been a scandal over this because Frank appears to have fled the country. … In Burma in the early 1920s, Eric was to meet his grandmother Limouzin, and presumably his Eurasian relatives – Aunt Aimée, daughter of William and Sooma, and his cousin, Kathleen, daughter of Frank and Mah Hlin, just four years older than himself. On this feature of his mother's family, he remained silent, but in his first novel, *Burmese Days*, he gave the name Ma Hla May to the Burmese mistress of his tragic hero John Flory.

Previous biographers had suggested that Eric Blair, aged five, was sent as a day boy to an Anglican convent in Henley. But Bowker argues convincingly that it was, in fact, a Catholic convent run by French Ursulines exiled from France after religious education was banned there in 1903 (p. 21). He concludes that if Blair was, then, first taught by Catholic nuns, this would explain two enduring aspects of his complex personality: 'his unremitting hostility towards Roman Catholicism and an acute sense of guilt' (ibid: 22).

Drawing from new correspondence with Steven Runciman, one of Orwell's friends at Eton (which he attended from 1917-1921), Bowker reveals the (perhaps surprising) fascination of Blair with the occult. A senior boy, Phillip Yorke, had attracted the disfavour of both Blair and Runciman so they planned a revenge.

> As Runciman recalled, they fashioned an image of Yorke from candle wax and broke off a leg. To their horror, shortly afterwards, Yorke not only broke his leg but in July died of leukaemia. The story of what happened soon spread and, in somewhat garbled form, became legend. Blair and Runciman suddenly found themselves regarded as distinctly odd, and to be treated warily (p. 56).

Previously unpublished letters between Orwell and one of his early female friends in Southwold, in the early 1930s, schoolteacher Brenda Salkeld, reveal other aspects of Orwell. He opens up to her, saying how depressed he is at the slow progress of his career and how at times he was losing confidence in himself as a writer (p. 125). 'Brenda noticed how he enjoyed trying to shock her with tales of his exploits in Burma and to offend her sense of delicacy with risqué stories and his collection of rude seaside postcards' (p. 124).

Bowker also harvested a lot of material, extracted from newly available KGB archives, on how Orwell was hunted and spied on while in Spain in 1937, fighting for the republicans against Franco's fascists in the Civil War. The man sent to Barcelona to spy for the KGB was David Crook whose reports on the Blairs (Orwell's newly-married wife, Eileen O'Shaughnessy, having joined him on the frontline) and his comrades George Kopp and John McNair were normally passed on to a Hugh O'Donnell, whose code name was O'Brien. As Bowker comments (p. 219):

> It seems unlikely that Orwell ever knew that Crook was spying on him, or that his contact worked under that name, but the fact that the character in *Nineteen Eighty-Four* who first wins the confidence of Winston Smith and then betrays him is given the name O'Brien must be one of the strangest coincidences in literature.

Towards the end of their time in Spain, in June 1937, the Blairs' flat in Hotel Continental, Barcelona, was raided by the Spanish secret police. All Orwell's diaries, press cuttings, letters to Eileen, fan letters about the recently published *The Road to Wigan Pier* and photographs were seized. Bowker adds (p. 222): 'Interestingly, one item taken, a French translation of Hitler's *Mein Kampf*, turned up in Crook's possession when he was arrested later on a trumped-up charge in connection with his spying activities.'

Following again Mumford's 'analytical, interpretative method', Bowker explores Orwell's personality in some depth. For instance, in discussing *The Road to Wigan Pier* (1937), his damning indictment of poverty, particularly among the miners, in northern England, Bowker highlights Orwell's obsession with dirt and foul smells: 'Stinks, stenches, reeks and odours of unimaginable repugnance swirl and permeate throughout his wretched worlds. … Orwell was repelled by filth and evil odours, but sought them out as if to rub his own nose in them to exorcise his demons through self-inflicted suffering' (pp 197-198).

Nor did Bowker shirk criticising his subject. Here, for instance, he suggests that *Wigan Pier*'s main weakness lay in Orwell's 'inability to portray working class life from the inside'. 'He later admitted that only a proletarian writer could get beyond the surface of proletarian life, but in an age when the bourgeoisie was the dominant class, proletarian writers had yet to find their own voice' (p. 198).

Elsewhere, Bowker highlights Orwell's obsession with lists: 'He made lists of books, redundant metaphors, jargon words, Kiplingesque epithets, poets who characterised the century and 'sentimental writers'. ... He was still constructing lists (and collecting junk) at the end of his life, most controversially the list of those he thought were suspected subversives' (p. 19).

Particularly impressive are the short commentaries on Orwell's writings dotted about the biography. Take, for instance, the six pages devoted to *Nineteen Eighty-Four* (pp 385-390). He begins by identifying the literary influences: Zamyatin, Trotsky, Jack London, Belloc, Poe and M. R. James. Orwell's horror at the Inquisition, his experience of terror in Spain and of the propaganda operation at the BBC, of wretched wartime London and the mysteries of junk shops are all there.

> The conundrum 2 + 2 = 5 was taken from Eugene Lyons writing about the Soviet Five Year Plan (it also crops up in *Tristram Shandy*). His fascination with the Chestertonian paradox is there in the form of 'Doublethink'. ... as is his identification with Protestant martyrs, his penchant for nursery rhymes, his fascination with fiction factories (offering formulae for novel writing) and the paranoia that led him to arm himself against possible assassination (p. 385).

Bowker next moves on to explore the religious sub-text. Many of the names of the characters in the novel are those of persecuted religious and political dissidents: 'Rutherford, Scottish dissident condemned to be burned, saved himself by confessing under torture; Jones, Chartist leader, persecuted and imprisoned for sedition; Tillotson, seventeenth-century preacher against popery; Wither and Ogilvy, Civil War turncoats' (p. 386).

The strange relationship with his previous novel, *Keep the Aspidistra Flying*, is next explored. 'Gordon Comstock is in advertising, sickened by the fact that he is paid to mislead and swindle the public; Winston Smith is in the business of misleading and swindling through deliberate falsification. *Keep the Aspidistra Flying* attacks the money-god, *Nineteen Eighty-Four* attacks the power-god' (p. 388). Bowker's interpretation of Julia, Smith's promiscuous lover, is also pleasantly controversial, raising the possibility that she was actually luring Smith into a honeytrap:

> Julia seems to be a secret hater of the Party and Big Brother, seems to be a candidate for the dissident Brotherhood, seems to go off to be tortured after her arrest and finally seems to have been purged of her thought-crime. But in the world of the book she could, like O'Brien and Charrington [the owner of the junk shop where the lovers conduct their secret affair], also

RICHARD LANCE KEEBLE

be a dissembler leading Winston straight into the arms of the Thought Police (ibid).

Bowker sums up astutely: 'On Airstrip One truth rests on ever-shifting sands, only pain and Room 101 are real. Such a reading gives the book a strangely modern character, making it a novel about the slippery, unstable nature of meaning' (ibid).

Such a section is so typical of this wonderful biography: it's incisive, original, elegantly written conveying – concisely – a vast knowledge of Orwell and the many influences on his personality and writings. And every time I re-read the biography it never ceases to give me such enormous pleasure. Thank you, Gordon.

- Gordon Bowker, who was born on 19 March 1934, wrote a number of other literary biographies: *Pursued by Furies: A Life of Malcolm Lowry* (1994) (*New York Times* Bestseller and Notable Book of the Year) and *Through the Dark Labyrinth: A Biography of Lawrence Durrell* (1996). His biography of James Joyce, published in May 2011 in time for Bloomsday, was longlisted for the Carnegie Medal for Literary Excellence, was the runner-up in 2013 for the American PEN/Jacqueline Bograd Weld Award for Biography and was shortlisted for the PEN Center USA West Literary Award. After reading English, Sociology and Philosophy at Nottingham and London Universities, he worked as a lecturer and wrote dramas and documentaries for radio and television. He contributed pieces to a wide variety of magazines and newspapers including *London Magazine*, *Plays and Players*, the *Listener*, *Sunday Times*, *Times Literary Supplement*, and *The New York Times*. He reported on the rise of the Polish trade union Solidarity for the *Illustrated London News*.

NOTE

[1] https://www.orwellfoundation.com/the-orwell-foundation/orwell/library/gordon-bowker-the-biography-orwell-never-wrote/

BOOK REVIEWS

Between the Bullet and the Lie: Essays on Orwell
Kristian Williams
AK Press, Chico CA, 2017, pp 271
ISBN 978 1 8493 5290 1 (pbk)

Kristian Williams's book-length collection of essays on Orwell is an interesting, entertaining and at times frustrating read. The author is an American anarchist intellectual who has written widely – in full-length books, pamphlets, essays, journalism, lectures and edited collections – about policing, counterinsurgency and the use of torture. If *Between the Bullet and the Lie* has the feel more of a collection of the author's already-extant work on Orwell than of a unitary book, this perhaps reflects the obviously contingent circumstances of some of these essays' writing. It also, though, makes it strangely moving to read – not as a series of purely critical engagements but as a record of a passionate engagement, spanning a life lived in work, in the library, in the meeting room and on the barricades. Williams divides the volume into two parts, one of 'Reflections on Orwell'; the other of 'Orwellian Reflections' – a playful arrangement that separates essays nominally focused on Orwell as a writer from those concerned with looking outwards, and applying his work to the contemporary world and attempts to change it.

Accordingly, *Between the Bullet and the Lie* is not a book of literary criticism but an instrumental work of political exegesis and reclamation, written by and for a reader whose engagement with Orwell intersects with their conscious involvement in political work. This can make it a challenging read at times for anyone more used to the hermeneutic procedures of academic reading. There are moments at which Williams's approach to the text seems rather more scriptural than critical: a particularly careful essay on Orwell's concept of 'decency' (pp 77-94), for example, undertakes a thorough enquiry into what Orwell really *meant* without ever quite admitting the possibility that that meaning may have been nebulous, or may have changed over time, or may have related to the word Orwell happened to use in sometimes fraught ways. This is, of course, not what the author is after, and it would be unfair to read *Between the Bullet and the Lie* as if it were supposed to be a work of literary scholarship. Williams writes with real passion about Orwell's strictures on writing, and quite emphatically endorses his dismissals of modernism; at times

– and this is intended as a compliment – reading his deployment of a thorough artistic, aesthetic and interpretative conservatism in the service of uncompromisingly radical politics can produce a feeling of exhilaration equal to that of encountering the same paradox in Orwell himself. Books as heavily invested as this one in Orwell's politics of expression – his anxiety that words should mean something, his horror of indeterminacy – usually tend to be written to claim him for the right, or at least against some notional idea of the postmodern left. So it is in some ways refreshing to see the revolutionary left use modes of argumentation – approachable, cautious and anti-theoretical – that it has largely abandoned.

However, this aversion to questions of textuality can lead on occasion to a failure to acknowledge Orwell's work as literature at all. In drawing out what he feels to be useful in Orwell's work and thought, Williams sometimes loses sight of the most basic deployments of literary artifice; the works become a rebus through which to access revealed truth, and ambiguity a minor obstacle on the way to resolution. Again, this is not supposed to be a book of textual criticism; but some attention to Orwell's literariness may have broadened and deepened the author's engagement, both with the works themselves and with their political potentialities. At certain points it is possible to see Williams and Orwell in a dialogue of which Williams seems quite unaware, and which may be as interesting for scholars of Orwell's reception as for activists interested in political readings and misreadings.

For example, neither Williams nor his subject seem anything but mystified by the possibility that language may have ritual or communal functions beyond mere signification, or that politics has an affectual and embodied content and practice; but Orwell's fiction comprehends these things quite thoroughly and Williams is an astute reader of it. There might be a productive tension to explore there, for a writer less inclined to take Orwell's line about prose 'like a pane of glass' quite so seriously as a directive.

If *Between the Bullet and the Lie* is a book about a body of texts which remains unconvinced of their textuality, it is also a book about their applicability to political life which bears a curiously oblique relationship to that life as it is now lived. The chapter entitled 'All but Hopeless: Pessimism in Politics' (pp 185-198) is one of the book's best, posing questions about how to keep radical hope alive, and how to continue to act and organise in the face of repeated defeats. Williams begins by noting that the grounds for optimism are scarce in a climate of global violence, climate change and looming resource scarcity, and laments that each successive social movement – anti-war, Occupy, Black Lives Matter – has collapsed or been crushed, leaving the participants to either despair or co-option. The anatomy he gives of the various kinds of despair and disillusionment that attend the unravelling of a hopeful radical moment is sharp, funny and uncomfortably accurate. 'Some years, or merely weeks, later,' he writes, ' – when the teargas has cleared, a few militants have been jailed, and some of the more ambitious leaders have settled into jobs with progressive non-profits or the Democratic Party – perhaps a few minor victories will have been won, but the ultimate aims seem as remote as ever' (p. 186). In some ways this sounds like the complaint of a typical post-war radical, accustomed to the numbing return of capitalist realism after every moment of prospective liberation, sure at least of the possibility of a return to a *status quo ante*, however ameliorated by minor reforms. To a reader in 2019 this seems impossibly distant: the liberal state has been hollowed out, capitalism faces a terminal planetary crisis, and it becomes less easy by the week to imagine the distant post-totalitarian or post-crisis future from which, like others, Williams imagines the Appendix to *Nineteen Eighty-Four* to have been written. It is possible that the two years which have elapsed since this book's publication have made a crucial difference, and that Williams would write a different book now; perhaps he is already doing so.

This crux, however, perhaps indicates some of the emergent political concerns to which Williams cannot quite make Orwell speak. The Anthropocene is one; the crisis of the nation is another. The second half of the book begins its application of Orwell to contemporary politics by considering 'Notes on Nationalism', *The Lion and the Unicorn* and *Coming Up for Air*, and attempting to parse the national determinants of Orwell's thought. 'Notes on Nationalism' is made to speak eloquently for itself, but the chapter as a whole seems curiously antiquated in its failure to interrogate the current position of the nation and the national community in global life and the political imaginary. Orwell's evocations of tea, heavy coins, bad teeth and cricket – like the equally sensual work of disgust and discomfort that Williams draws attention to in *The Road to Wigan Pier* and *Nineteen Eighty-Four* – have powerful valence in interrogating the affective, experiential, embodied and mnemonic bases of political community and belonging, on the one hand, and abjection and alienation on the other. Here, as previously, it is hard not to think that, for all Williams's dismissive hostility to intellectualised 'identity politics' and academic life, a less conservative textual approach may have improved the book's yield of usable political insights.

The book's final few pages reflect powerfully on the cultural and political legacies of the Spanish Civil War, quoting both Orwell's 'violent resentment at having to leave this world which … suits me so well' upon being shot in Spain in 1937, and the similar sentiments in the final scene of Hemingway's *For Whom the Bell Tolls* (1940): the 'world is a fine place and worth fighting for and

REVIEW

I hate very much to leave it' (pp 207-208). The business of living in the Anthropocene makes these lines read somewhat differently, just as it troubles the narrative framework of return and resurgence with which, in this case, Williams invokes the persistence of Spain in the political imagination; and just as it troubles, on a more universal scale, the whole basis of linear historical time which these essays, like Orwell's writings, inhabit.

None of this, of course, is to say that *Between the Bullet and the Lie* fails as a serious engagement with Orwell. It does not. That it should be difficult to know how to review this book for an academic journal reflects badly only upon academia. Academia must bear some of the blame, too, for the implicit distinction between 'textual' and 'useful' criticism which seems to undergird, and at times, undermine Williams's readings. *Between the Bullet and the Lie* is still a useful book and, at its best, does direct, political and necessary work that scholarship ought to be ashamed it does not do itself.

Peter Mitchell,
University of Manchester

George Orwell on Screen
David Ryan
McFarland, Jefferson, NC, 2018, pp 246
ISBN 978 1 4766 7369 1 (print); 978 1 4766 8 (ebook)

I remember noting the name David Ryan a couple of years ago when *The Road to Wigan Pier: A Musical Documentary* was shown at the NFT. At the time, I took him for either one of those spotters of Orwell arcana or a really good BFI researcher. There has now appeared an intriguing and magnificently researched book by the same David Ryan on film and television adaptations of George Orwell's works.

Ryan does not just scrutinise the films but also raises questions about how we interpret the texts. In the process, he demonstrates that filming Orwell has much to do with the filmmaker's vision and willingness to experiment with form. As A. L. Kennedy notes in the Introduction, the book also offers 'an oblique record of decline in television production standards' (p. 2). The intent and achievements of the early pioneers of television drama on both sides of the Atlantic are praised, unlike today's mass of docudramas with their fifteen-minute sections all neatly demarcated with points repeated at strategic intervals.

Ryan's approach is to look at the circumstances behind the productions, how the work was adapted and the critical responses. There is no overt theorising: Ryan is first and foremost a journalist. Each decade from the 1950s onwards is given its respective section allowing its own mode of interpretation to be analysed: the CIA-backed adaptations of the '50s, the narrative experiments of the '60s and the various representations of *Nineteen Eighty-Four* in the '80s.

BBC drama in the '60s was often recorded on videotape, much of which would be then wiped for subsequent programmes. This was the case for three Orwell productions from 1965: *Keep the Aspidistra Flying*, *Coming Up for Air* and *Nineteen Eighty-Four*. While no production stills are available for these films, Ryan is able to quote from their scripts, by Robin Chapman. The documentaries of the '70s and '80s survive, only just, thanks to YouTube or, as noted above, BFI showings. The earlier works from the 1960s and '70s benefit from showing living witnesses recording their memories: 'proud, articulate, self-educated trade unionists dressed in their Sunday best with a bookcase full of hardbacks' (p. 97) alongside the usual suspects of Richard Rees, Cyril Connolly and the occasional surprise such as Norman Mailer, interviewed by Melvyn Bragg in 1971. The other documentary of the 1970s, *The Road to Wigan Pier: A Musical Documentary* (1973) serves as a key example of why Ryan's book is necessary. Made by Canadian expatriate Frank Cvitanovich, the one-hour film mixes readings by Michael Jayston with folk songs by Bob Davenport. It offers a very different, and also very welcome, documentary to the usual talking-heads pieces. It is also one of the least-known Orwell films and may have passed us all by if not for Ryan's championing of it.

REVIEW

Ryan's analysis of the 1997 version of *Keep the Aspidistra Flying* offers a more forensic examination of this film than it probably warrants. Alan Plater's screenplay for *The Crystal Spirit* is one of the key pieces of Orwellian drama: a moving depiction of the time Orwell spent on Jura writing *Nineteen Eighty-Four*. After this success, Plater was commissioned to write the screenplay for *Keep the Aspidistra Flying* – but it was hugely disappointing.

Then there is the big beast itself: *Nineteen Eighty-Four*. Seven of the twenty-one productions discussed are either of the book or relate to its creation – from a CBS one-hour production in 1953 through to Michael Radford's 1984 film. Ryan guides us through the basics of the commissioning procedure and the production issues and even offers some myth-busting assessments of the public impact various adaptations had. The public and critical reviews collected in this chapter reveal a country unsure of what to make of this new medium, intrigued by the possibilities of the screen in the room but also angry at what could be shown.

There is sadly no image of David Buck in the 1965 BBC production but there are of the other actors who have played Winston. Each reveals something of the production: for instance, Eddie Albert (Irish-American working-class), Peter Cushing (emaciated aesthete) and Edmond O'Brien (middleweight boxer/prop forward).

Most of these films or TV productions are ones with which we should probably be more familiar and it sad to note just how many require the BFI or digital support to be seen again. In some respects, this book should act as a call to arms encouraging our broadcast companies to repeat, or the BFI to release, suitable compilations of Orwell-related work.

Simon Goulding,
Independent scholar

The Politics of 1930s British Literature: Education, Class, Gender

Natasha Periyan
Bloomsbury, London, 2018, pp 278
ISBN 978 2 3500 1984 3 (hbk)

It is perhaps evidence of an academic tendency to repress the pedagogical that a book like Natasha Periyan's *The Politics of 1930s British Literature: Education, Class, Gender* has not come to light until now. As Periyan points out, critical works citing the relationship between education and the literary 1930s too easily concede that allusions to pedagogy are merely allegories for broader, and purportedly more important, cultural debates over the tenor of political rhetoric. In other words, references to education in the inter-war period have never been understood literally, but always as a stand-in for discussions about polemical strategy. As such, criticism within the field addressing the intersection of inter-war literature and education repeatedly overlooks the conjunctions between the *realpolitik* of educational policy and writers' acute investments in vibrant debates over educational reform.

Periyan's book corrects this oversight and, in so doing, broadens the scope of 'thirties' literature. Rather than defining the period through international political commitments (i.e., Valentine Cunningham's foregrounding of the Spanish Civil War), the book frames the thirties through the intersection of British literature and domestic efforts to expand the scope of secondary education. The book positions the 1926 Hadow Report, which advocated for an expansion of the school leaving age to fifteen, as the first of several egalitarian Labour proposals on education. Though many proposed reforms met frustration at the hand of Conservatives, the calls for change continued, and only increased in volume throughout the inter-war period. By re-envisioning British inter-war literature through the lens of localised controversy, Periyan provides an overdue recognition that international discussions about liberty and equality had domestic parallels as well.

Periyan asserts that inter-war debates about the future of educational access strongly corresponded with theories of how to produce a more just, democratic society in Britain, more inclusive of women and the working classes. Addressing at every turn the myriad ways in which practical educational reform emerged in inter-war writings, Periyan surveys an impressive array of writers and the impact of educational reform on their aesthetics, including W. H. Auden, Stephen Spender, Vera Brittain, Winifred Holtby, Graham Greene, Arthur Calder-Marshall, Antonia White, Virginia Woolf, Henry Green, Cyril Connolly and George Orwell.

A testament to both the importance of the historically-minded formalism of New Modernist Studies and the revived interest in an expansive 1930s, the book's thesis – that many writers of the inter-war were 'engaged with contemporary debates surrounding educational expansion' – is supported by an impressive array of archival research (p. 16). For example, Periyan bolsters her analysis of *South Riding* through the introduction of Holtby's unpublished political writings on secondary education, even looking to her editorial changes as evidence of an increasingly critical perspective on the exclusion of women in the educational field. In several instances, Periyan dissects the evolution of manuscripts diachronically to trace shifts in authors' views on education and politics. This most clearly emerges in her analysis of the unpopular changes in the final scene of Auden's *The Dog Beneath the Skin*, where she contends that Auden's emendations attempted to balance his critique of educational conservatism with his desire to maintain an undogmatic approach to his audience. This genetically-informed methodological approach, looking across both time and genre, materialises the dynamism of both educational policy and literary style in the period.

REVIEW

The extensive list of writers surveyed leads Periyan to group them in new and compelling ways. Chapter three presents the most striking example of this, as it describes at least five authors featured in Graham Greene's *The Old School*, a collection of essays where authors reflected on their own educational experiences. This chapter most clearly embodies Periyan's claim that progressive theories of educational reform, with their emphasis on collective politics, can emerge unexpectedly via literary form. The varied and divergent voices of the sixteen contributors to *The Old School* attest to the importance of collectivity as both a literary form and an educational model; the inclusive changes to education suggested in contributors' essays mirrored the inclusion of diverse voices in the edited collection itself. Other chapters develop more author-based approaches, like those on Auden and Woolf. Still others adopt fitting partnerships or groupings of authors. The chapter on Winifred Holtby and Vera Brittain cites their friendship and political involvement in the National Union of Women Teachers as evidence of the pair's commitments to the expansion of women's roles in education as both students and teachers.

In the chapter addressing Cyril Connolly, Henry Green and George Orwell, Periyan looks to the writers' deployment of rhetoric and dialect to assert that the literary style of Etonian writers is 'formulated in both response and resistance to' the privilege of their educational experiences (p. 187). Her analysis of Orwell, primarily centred on *The Road to Wigan Pier*, argues that the 'mercurial, ventriloquial, and rhetorical' style of the text contributes to the effectiveness of Orwell's class-conscious political critique (p. 188). Reading carefully his use of inverted commas, the subjunctive, passive construction, and his sardonic arguments about class division, Periyan counters common critiques of *Wigan Pier* (particularly by Victor Gollancz), which claim that the book's second section fails to bridge the gap between the author's privileged experience and the working-class one he describes. Periyan's recuperative analysis notes that Orwell's indeterminate style destabilises the authoritarian qualities typically affiliated with the educated upper-classes; the chapter sees Orwell's ventriloquism of the working-class acting in concert with, not in opposition to, his more 'sophisticated' style through a deliberate rhetorical method intended to critique class prejudice.

The concluding chapter on the Etonian writers underscores a dominant theme throughout the book: the increasing importance of discourses around working-class education in the 1930s. For many, educational reforms proffered a post-war opportunity to embrace an egalitarian society and relax class boundaries. The increasing rancour around education and growing popularity of universal educational access, as Periyan describes in the Introduction, lend her readings of the 1930s a new significance and demonstrate how educational debates informed literary style. This book is highly recommended for scholars of the inter-war period and beyond, as Periyan's intervention sheds new light on the intersectionality of everyday politics and literary form throughout the twentieth century.

Megan Faragher,
Wright State University, Lake Campus

George Orwell Illustrated

David Smith, Mike Mosher (illus.)
Haymarket Books, Chicago, 2018, pp 267
ISBN 978 1 6084 6783 9 (pbk)

REVIEW

George Orwell Illustrated is a curious book. Ostensibly an 'updated and expanded edition' of the 1984 *Orwell for Beginners*, it features the reprint of that earlier text and a new section entitled 'Planet Orwell' which seeks to argue for the continuing relevance of Orwell's writings in 2018 (the year of publication). I say the book is curious for several reasons, but here I will focus on two: quite simply, audience and venue.

As for audience, we must look at the original 'For Beginners' series which *George Orwell Illustrated* updates (Haymarket Books has done the same with David Smith's *Marx's* Capital *for Beginners*, now *Marx's* Capital *Illustrated*). I remember this series, having owned and read *Einstein for Beginners* when I was 12 or 13, and I will admit that my own flimsy grasp on quantum theory owes a debt to that book. They were ideal, like many of the 'Dummies' and 'Idiot's' guides which followed, for interested non-specialists. They were also a product of their time: most were produced in the late-1970s/early-1980s, on the cusp of the personal computing boom, capturing in print the promise of multimedia presentations of information at your fingertips. This is, of course, not to argue for the obsolescence of illustrated texts today, but rather situate the originally-intended logic and audience for this book in what was a very different publishing market. I key into this issue of audience because the reasons for its reprint seem based in the material supplied in 'Planet Orwell' which, itself, is not mainly for an audience of interested non-specialists.

This raises the question of venue. The book's selling point is, akin to the 'previously unreleased tracks' sales pitch of an album re-release, advertised as a 'discovery' of a 'human rights manifesto co-authored with Bertrand Russell and Arthur Koestler …[which] appears here for the first time'. All this is, as they say, 'huge if true'. However, most of the words from that back cover description are wrong or misleading. The phrase 'human rights' is never used in the document (instead, 'rights of man'); the document was never titled and Orwell called it a 'draft manifesto' once, adding 'or whatever it is' in a letter to Koestler (Orwell 2001 [1998]: 28); it was not lost and waiting to be discovered, but catalogued in at least two archives – and Peter Davison's summary of its contents in the *Complete Works* mirrors the original language so closely, he evidently had access to it (ibid: 7). But it is fair to say that this is the first publication of a particular document.

Why am I being so precise? Partly because the authorship of what appears in *George Orwell Illustrated* is contestable, partly because of the uncorroborated claim that Arthur Koestler and Bertrand Russell signed the document, partly because there are unexplained changes between the surviving copies of the document and the published version, and partly because it is being presented as a key selling point for the book.

The book publishes a document mailed to Ruth Fischer from Arthur Koestler in 1949 and held in her papers at Harvard University (pp 230-234). But it is not the only copy, as the book definitely wants you to believe. The Centre for Research Collections at the University of Edinburgh has eight copies of this document as part of the Arthur Koestler archive, two of which contain marginal notes, and all of which contain distinctly different stapling marks, suggesting these copies were sent out to different correspondents and subsequently returned. We know from the surviving correspondence between Koestler, Orwell and others that a draft of a petition was being circulated for comment and that Koestler seems to have been collecting the comments (Orwell op cit: 7, 8, 28, 105, 133). There is also a letter in that same file from Victor Gollancz adding his comments. None of this material is filed with Orwell's letter containing the original draft he sent Koestler. This first draft survives but was for some unexplained reason not included in the *Complete Works*. The document Koestler sent Ruth Fischer years later, which Smith publishes, regardless of how Koestler represented it to her, is identical to the eight copies in the Koestler archive. There are unexplained changes made by Smith in the published text and, despite his claim of Koestler's and Russell's signature on the Fischer copy, none of the copies are signed at all, nor does Smith share where he got this particular detail. The changes Smith introduces are often small, but there are at least two which alter meaning in the text, and whether or not the new paragraph breaks he introduces are meaningful could be subject to debate. There is clearly much to indicate multiple unacknowledged hands on this text before its publication.

Essentially, there are three surviving versions of this document: the first draft Orwell sent Koestler on 2 January 1946; an excerpt from this was modified by Koestler and included in his 10 March 1946 *New York Times Magazine* article 'Challenge to Russia: Lift the Iron Curtain!', which Smith partly reproduces (pp 238-240); and the revision Koestler sent Fisher (and others), which is printed in *George Orwell Illustrated*. The *New York Times Magazine* article refers neither to Orwell nor the plans for a new organisation, and Koestler does not appear to have mentioned the article's existence to Orwell – Smith says Koestler 'adapted' Orwell's draft (p. 238), but I believe there is a plagiarism case to be made. Koestler's hand is so strong in this sequence of events it could be argued that what gets printed as Orwell's manifesto should more rightly considered Koestler's.

REVIEW

The correspondence in the *Complete Works* shows that Orwell saw the revision and there is no account of him objecting to it. However, it differs so greatly from Orwell's first draft that they could properly be considered different texts, and should be subjected to a side-by-side comparative analysis. Smith does mention having access to 'excerpts' of this draft, which he quotes, but it raises the question why he did not bother consulting the Koestler archive which possesses a complete copy (p. 236). Some of what is at issue is how Smith's archival research was performed, what conclusions he drew, and how he presented them. The sourcing for Smith's tale of how the manifesto was drafted, circulated, discussed and revised is somewhat unclear. The descriptions of the interpersonal dynamics seem to be shaped by Koestler's accounts of events with some supplementing with the *Complete Works*. As the authorship of these documents is at issue, a more transparent process would be called for. For example, could the editor of the Bertrand Russell papers of the late-1940s claim this as a co-authored Russell document? Does the claim of Russell's signature permit this?

A fuller examination of this document and the history of its production is clearly required. Smith's version of events – the sources for which he supplies through a link to ResearchGate, which unfortunately requires an account, login, and then a request to access the document – makes it clear he only ever considered the Ruth Fischer archive for drafts of this document. In his notes, Smith declares that several of the notable facts cited above, 'like the manifesto itself, appear in only one of three three [sic] places – Fischer's archive, here, and *George Orwell Illustrated*' (Smith 2018: 7). As regards to what he calls the manifesto, this is demonstrably inaccurate and again raises serious questions about research method. It is not to say Smith is in error throughout, but as the typo in the quote above hints at, there has been a certain lack of care about getting this story right.

To be fair, Smith attempts a kind of contextualisation, envisioning the document as a triangulation of Orwell's, Koestler's and Russell's concerns at the time (pp 228-240). But that manoeuvre assumes much about authorship and ignores much of the specificity of Orwell's world in late 1945-early 1946. It strikes me that much more consideration should have been given to Orwell's reading of H. G. Wells's *Rights of Man* – the correspondence shows he has it on his mind in relation to this document (Orwell op cit: 28) – and Orwell's suspicion of the National Council for Civil Liberties (which is named in the published version (p. 231)), as well as taking his involvement in the Freedom Defence Committee more seriously. And in my opinion, the key missing detail in all of this is Orwell's critical distance from PEN, an organisation which had very much been on his mind at the time and which had approached him to join in a leadership capacity early in 1946, and of which Koestler was a member (Orwell op cit: 138). In short, it is, indeed, a rich find but it deserves a lot more scholarly attention.

I have made such a point about this one element of the book largely because it has been promoted as the reason to buy it. If the reader is looking for recent studies of Orwell's political thought, I would steer them towards John Newsinger's *Hope Lies in the Proles* (2018) and David Dwan's *Liberty, Equality and Humbug: Orwell's Political Ideals* (2018). Smith's book may not be for the reader of *George Orwell Studies*, but all the more reason to get it right for a broader audience.

REFERENCES

Orwell, George (2001 [1998]) *The Complete Works of George Orwell, Vol. 18: Smothered Under Journalism, 1946*, Davison, Peter (ed.) London: Secker & Warburg

Smith, Mike (2018) George Orwell documented: References and art credits for *George Orwell Illustrated*, Available online at https://www.researchgate.net/publication/328890586_George_Orwell_Documented_References_and_art_credits_for_George_Orwell_Illustrated, accessed on 1 March 2019

Matthew Chambers,
University of Warsaw

RE-EVALUATIONS

Tombs: Sharing Orwell's Penchant for Puncturing Shibboleths

DARCY MOORE

George Orwell continues to have an extraordinary influence on how the English view England, writes Darcy Moore in his review of an important contemporary work of history.

The English and Their History: The First Thirteen Centuries (2014) by Robert Tombs has deservingly been described as a 'triumph', 'magisterial' and 'astonishing' by reviewers. The historian has been praised for being 'shrewdly detached' and writing with 'precision and candour'. There is plenty of support for the view this will be 'the standard history for years' (see, for instance, Davenport-Hines 2014; Hitchens 2015, Mullin 2015).

Tombs wants to tell the history of England 'first as an idea, and then as a kingdom, as a country, a people and a culture, trying to begin at the beginning without assuming any inevitability in what occurred, and trying to explore what is proper to England, and what is shared with its various neighbours'. Although he wanted 'to reflect the best modern scholarship, much of it hidden from the public gaze in the pages of learned journals and scholarly monographs', Tombs makes no use of contemporary DNA analysis or population genetics in his chronological narrative (Tombs 2014: 17). It has been pointed out, by one reviewer, that Tombs's index has no reference to regionalism, class, gender or race (Colley 2015). He argues:

> …it is meaningless to attempt any description of a society – that it was rich or poor, equal or unequal, free or oppressed, stable or unstable – except by comparison with other human societies (ibid: 20).

Contextually, this history was published before the Brexit referendum of June 2016 and two months after the Scots voted 'no' in response to the question: 'Should Scotland be an independent country?'. Tombs describes himself as 'an Englishman with Irish connections who has spent most of his life studying France' and says his 'approach to England's history has necessarily been without fixed preconceptions and, explicitly or implicitly, it is constantly concerned with wider historical perspectives' (ibid: 20).

Tombs is no invisible, disinterested academic silently working with the archives and intellectual theory. He was critical of the National Curriculum for History and was invited to help rewrite it by the Secretary of State, Michael Gove, in 2013 (Tombs 2017a). As co-founder of the *Briefings for Brexit* website, which aims to provide 'factual evidence and reasoned arguments', Tombs believes, 'whatever the theorists say, ordinary people seem intuitively to feel the opposite: they look for security to the people they know and trust, and to governments over which they have some direct control. That is what Brexit means' (Tombs 2017b).

Like Orwell, Tombs is critical of 'smelly little orthodoxies'. Unlike Orwell, he appears to have no fondness for left wing or progressive politics. He presents a persuasive amount of data to argue the period of the 1960s was destructive for English society and one reviewer notices he can rarely 'mention any Labour politician without sarcasm' (Colley 2015).

THE INFLUENCE OF GEORGE ORWELL

A text search for 'Orwell', in the Kindle edition of Tombs's single-volume history, reveals the author is referenced thirty-one times throughout the thousand-page monograph. It is hardly surprising Shakespeare garners seventy-six references and Dickens forty-eight. T. S. Eliot and Jane Austen languish with four and seven references respectively.

Historians such as the Venerable Bede, Geoffrey of Monmouth, A. J. P. Taylor, E. P. Thompson and Christopher Hill are all referred to far less than Orwell. Edward Gibbon is mentioned just three times and Eric Hobsbawm even less. David Hume and Thomas Babington Macaulay are employed a few more times in the service Tombs's narrative than Orwell but Winston Churchill, who had the advantage of being historian, journalist, author and twice prime minister, dwarfs all others with nearly two-hundred references.

Orwell's fiction is not mentioned at all. Not one allusion to Airstrip One, Oceania, Newspeak, Big Brother or Manor Farm is to be found. This makes sense as Tombs says:

> Historical novelists, playwrights or film-makers may feel free to tell the story however they wish; but historians are guided and indeed constrained by this research, which dictates much of what can and must be written (ibid: 17).

However, a select number of Orwell's most important writings – 'Shooting an Elephant' (1936), 'Boys' Weeklies' (1939), 'Charles Dickens' (1940) and *The Lion and the Unicorn* (1941) – are significant to Tombs's telling of his story of the English. One of Orwell's standard published works is referenced too, *The Road to Wigan Pier* (1937). These non-fiction evaluations of aspects of English life and culture are invaluable to Tombs's vision.

It struck me several times that Tombs has an Orwellian gift for writing, not so much epithets but amusingly acerbic sentences that one would usually associate with bias, or at the least, opinion pieces. However, just when one is tempted to view Tombs's history as a partisan, rather than balanced work, he delights with a reference, quote or insight that helps one back on the road to believing, if not being completely convinced, he is fair-minded and independent. Tombs eventually convinced this sceptical reader, although my inner critic was poised and ready to doubt, that his historical judgement was sound.

One example where I struggled, albeit relatively briefly, was when Tombs creatively employs Orwell in an apparent defence of imperialism by quoting from 'Shooting an Elephant', followed by *The Lion and the Unicorn* – along with Edward Said's *Culture and Imperialism* (1993):

> But they did bring substantial periods of relative peace and order to large tracts of the globe – in the view of the same Orwell, 'the Empire was peaceful as no area of comparable size has ever been' (ibid: 781).

He argues that one benefit of this imperial legacy was that the English language 'made the world one' (ibid: 782). This very much follows his belief that one can only judge any society by 'comparison with other human societies' (ibid: 20).

Tombs shares Orwell's penchant for puncturing shibboleths. He writes cleverly and coherently to create a surprising amount of order from 'a confused mass of ideas' and adheres successfully to Orwell's dictum about good prose and window panes:

> As a subject of academic study memory was first undertaken by French historians, whose term mémoire suggests not individual recollections but what is sometimes called 'social memory' – a public culture, recorded in monuments, books, institutions and symbols. This book pursues that idea: the history of England is not simply what happened, or what historians believe they can demonstrate, but what a vast range of people, for a great variety of purposes, have recorded, asserted and believed about the past – a confused mass of ideas, emotions, words and images, often contradictory, argumentative and divisive (Tombs 2014: 17).

> A good example of this can be seen in Orwell's observation that the beloved novelist, Charles Dickens, 'attacked English institutions with a ferocity that has never since been approached. Yet he managed to do so without making himself hated and he has become a national institution' (ibid: 424).

It is noteworthy that Tombs is more than happy to write about Dickens through Orwell's eyes.

Indeed, the most English of Englishmen, George Orwell, greatly valued his French ancestry and was very knowledgeable about French literature, especially poetry. Tombs's academic specialisation is French History. By the time I had finished his book, it felt that the spectre of Orwell loomed larger than any other figure influencing and confirming Tombs's perspective on England. It was easy to imagine Orwell reviewing this book approvingly. It is also possible to imagine Tombs's disappointment that the planned epic poem, the one that would have explored the history of England in a way Orwell described as 'Chaucerian' to a friend, was left unwritten at his death.

THE ENGLISH AND THEIR HISTORY: CONCLUSION

The influence of Orwell on Tombs's thinking is most evident in the concluding chapter which opens with a quote from *The Lion and The Unicorn*:

> Nothing ever stands still. We must add to our heritage or lose it, we must grow greater or grow less, we must go forward or backward. I believe in England, and I believe that we shall go forward (Tombs 2014: 873).

In many ways it is not surprising that Tombs has chosen Orwell's most optimistic book, written during 'The Blitz', as a seminal text informing and explaining his own historical perspective. His thinking and writing overtly employ Orwell's language and imagery. Tombs uses the analogy of a *house* in a similar manner to Orwell's famous description of England as a *family*:

> Nations resemble each other like a street of houses: of different sizes, with different occupants, and different furnishings, but sharing many basic characteristics. England is a rambling old property with ancient foundations, a large Victorian extension, a 1960s garage, and some annoying leaks and draughts balancing its period charm. Some historians believe England to be the prototype of the nation-state: 'The birth of the English nation was not the birth of a nation; it was the birth of the nations' (Tombs 2014: 873).

Tombs understands that collective memory, as a pillar of national identity, values the 'shared possession of a rich heritage of memories at its heart' (ibid: 17). One senses that Orwell is very much part of this house and it is amusing to think that *The Lion and the Unicorn*, sub-titled 'Socialism and the English Genius', would sit comfortably on the mantelpiece alongside Tombs's work. One senses that his description of this book – as Orwell's 'exasperated love letter to England' – could easily be a reference to Tombs's own monograph (ibid: 697). Orwell's image, of the photograph on the mantelpiece, is a particularly powerful one for Tombs:

> George Orwell's view was typically trenchant: 'What can the England of 1940 have in common with the England of 1840? But then, what have you in common with the child of five whose photograph your mother keeps on the mantelpiece? Nothing, except that you happen to be the same person.' The connection, he said, was that 'it is your civilisation, it is you…' (Tombs 2014: 880).

RE-EVALUATION

Tombs mentions that George Orwell was 'not being controversial' in commenting in 1940 on the 'gentleness of English civilisation … You notice it the instant you set foot on English soil' (ibid: 790). It is clear that Tombs, like Orwell, knows the high value of trust and believes that the English people still possess this quality so essential to the national identity of what Daniel Defoe called, a 'mongrel race':

> … opinion polls suggest that English feelings of national identity today are strong, and very similar to those of their close European neighbours. According to one critical observer, 'It is necessary for peoples to trust each other, and somehow the English still do.' They show it in public outrage when trust is betrayed by politicians. This, however little boasted about, is a quality beyond price (ibid: 884-885).

Tombs acknowledges the obvious truth that 'every work of history reflects the experiences, beliefs and personality of its writer' and has demonstrated, throughout his lengthy narrative, that good historians, like himself, are guided and constrained by their research 'which dictates much of what can and must be written' (Tombs 2014: 17).

In many ways Orwell is like that *house* Tombs employs as an analogy for England; complex, paradoxical, ramshackle, more than a little leaky and certainly not built to plan. Orwell was an imperial police officer, democratic socialist, Tory anarchist and radical. He was also a man who liked flowers, especially roses, tea and English pubs. An intellectual, he liked working with his hands. He hated imperialism, censorship and propaganda but was prepared to serve during World War II at the BBC as a broadcaster 'talking to India', influencing people he believed should be free of the imperial yolk to be committed to the British empire. Orwell flirted with pacifism but was badly wounded in the fight against fascism. An atheist all his adult life, he was buried after a traditional Anglican service. He was English (but more than a little French and Scottish).

Tombs believes in England. One can easily imagine Orwell evaluating this as history written by a patriot, seeing things as they truly are, rather than an intellectual 'ashamed of their own nationality'. Tombs, one also imagines, would enjoy such a judgement a great deal.

REFERENCES

Briefings for Brexit (2019) Available online at https://briefingsforbrexit.com/, accessed on 22 February 2019

Colley, Linda (2015) A shared island, *Times Literary Supplement*, 7 January. Available online at https://www.the-tls.co.uk/articles/public/a-shared-island/, accessed on 22 February 2019

Davenport-Hines, Richard (2014) *The English and Their History* review – 'a book of resounding importance to contemporary debates', *Guardian*, 17 November. Available online at https://www.theguardian.com/books/2014/nov/17/the-english-and-their-history-review-robert-tombs-resounding-importance, accessed on 15 February 2019

Hitchens, Peter (2015) *The English and Their History*, by Robert Tombs, *New York Times*, 31 December. Available online at https://www.nytimes.com/2016/01/03/books/review/the-english-and-their-history-by-robert-tombs.html, accessed on 15 February 2019

Mullin, Chris (2015) *The English and Their History*, by Robert Tombs, *Irish Times*, 1 February. Available online at https://www.irishtimes.com/culture/books/the-english-and-their-history-by-robert-tombs-1.2084518, accessed on 22 February 2019

Ltd.

Tombs, Robert (2014) *The English and Their History: The First Thirteen Centuries*, Penguin Books Ltd. Kindle Edition

Tombs, Robert (2017a) Why Teach Your Own Country's History? *parentsandteachers.org.uk*, 9 March. Available online at http://www.parentsandteachers.org.uk/latest/blog/why-teach-your-own-countrys-history-speech-professor-robert-tombs, accessed on 23 February 2019

Tombs, Robert (2017b) Brexit suggests we're on the right side of history, *Spectator*, 16 December. Available online at https://www.spectator.co.uk/2017/12/brexit-suggests-were-on-the-right-side-of-history/, accessed on 22 February 2019

George Orwell Studies

Subscription information
Each volume contains two issues, published half-yearly.

Annual Subscription (including postage)

Personal Subscription

UK	£25
Europe	£28
RoW	£30

Institutional Subscription

UK	£100
Europe	£115
RoW	£120

Single Issue copies (subject to availability)

UK	£15
Europe	£17
RoW	£20

Enquiries regarding subscriptions and orders should be sent to:

Journals Fulfilment Department
Abramis Academic
ASK House
Northgate Avenue
Bury St Edmunds
Suffolk, IP32 6BB
UK

Tel: +44(0)1284 700321
Email: info@abramis.co.uk

www.ingramcontent.com/pod-product-compliance
Lightning Source LLC
Chambersburg PA
CBHW080406170426
43193CB00016B/2834